D1416473

Rough Diamonds

Rough Diamonds
A Coach's Journey

Tommy Reamon
with Ron Whitenack

Forewords by Michael Vick
and Nikki Giovanni

TRIUMPH
B O O K S
CHICAGO

This book is available in quantity at special discounts for your group or organization. For further information, contact:

Triumph Books
601 South LaSalle Street
Suite 500
Chicago, Illinois 60605
(312) 939-3330
Fax (312) 663-3557

Printed in the United States of America
ISBN 1-57243-568-2

Edited and produced by Through the Moon Editorial and Publishing Services, P.O. Box 175, Hillsborough, North Carolina, 27278, info@throughthemoon.com.

Dedication

I wish to dedicate this book to my mother, Nettie Elizabeth Watkins Reamon Pierce—you have always been my best friend.

To my son, Tommy Jr., who truly is my second heartbeat and the ultimate diamond in my life.

To all the players I have enjoyed coaching over the years and shared a special relationship with . . . you know who you are.

My special thanks to La Verne Katherine Jackson Warthen.

Contents

Foreword

by Michael Vick

If you are a high school football fanatic like I was, you will need a coach like Tommy Reamon to help you realize your dream of becoming a top professional like me. Coach Reamon was like a father to me in high school. He kind of took me under his wing and molded me. He taught me a lot of things about life as well as football, and we were always talking about my responsibilities as a player and a person. When I look back on our relationship, Coach poured his soul into me to make sure that I didn't make some of the mistakes that he made in his college and professional years. He made sure that I kept the proper perspective and developed the necessary tools to cope with the enormous attention I would get both on and off the field.

When I first met Coach Reamon, I told him that I wanted him to help me get a football scholarship to college just like he did for my cousin Aaron Brooks. He promised he would if I did everything he asked of me. Well, I tried, and he had input about everything, even where he thought I should go to school. He knew I could be good in the Syracuse system, but he knew I'd be *better* at Virginia Tech. He told me that about twenty times, and it began to sink in.

Coach Reamon had a sixth sense about my future and the things that would happen to me, and the confidence he worked so hard to instill in me became very clear one evening as he and my mother sat in room 2501 of New York City's Downtown Athletic Club. Two hours earlier I had become only the third freshman ever to finish in the top three in the Heisman Trophy balloting. As we happily shared the moment, I told them that I was just overwhelmed by all of this. My mother said, "Michael, when I watch you play ball, I'm like, 'Who is that? This is all a dream.'" Then suddenly, Coach says, "It's a dream, but it was also planned. Decisions were made a long time ago that made this night possible. Michael, this is just the beginning." After Coach Reamon's statement, it became clear to me that he was living his dreams through me, so it became important to me to dream and strive for the success of both of us. I'm proud to say that I wouldn't be where I am without the help of Coach Reamon. Therefore, every aspiring high school football player should read this book so that he will know what ingredients go into the making of a top-quality coach. Good luck, and enjoy the journey.

Michael Vick
Quarterback, Atlanta Falcons
Atlanta, Georgia

Foreword
"Diamonds in the Rough: Hold On"

by Nikki Giovanni

This is for the men . . . the men with hopes and dreams and talents . . . that sometimes other men find ways to use and use and use up . . . and when the men are used up they are discarded . . . like so many Christmas toys that don't work or maybe like Easter eggs that have teeny tiny cracks . . . not enough cracks so that the Easter Bunny and his crew refuse to dye them . . . they . . . after all . . . look so lovely when scattered across the lawn in all their many colors but . . . well . . . that teeny tiny crack is just enough to sort of say *sure you can find this pretty egg and maybe put it in your basket for a while but don't you know that little crack means one day it will stink* . . . that one day whatever it is that makes eggs break open . . . whatever it is that snuggles inside . . . whatever it is that wants . . . needs . . . has . . . to get out . . . will break this shell causing a stink . . . this is for the men

This is for the men . . . the men who knew the difference between cutting bait . . . and fishing . . . and who having been carted away from all known waters . . . found a way to fish . . . anyway . . . like the women found a way . . . to quilt . . . like we all found a way . . . to maintain integrity . . . this is for the men who were sent back . . . for a reason . . . or no reason . . . this is for the men who

ran . . . and tackled . . . and threw their bodies
. . . to block the way . . . and no body ever really
said Thank You . . . no everybody assumed . . .
this made them happy . . . never ever knowing what
makes men happy . . . other men claimed some kind
of right . . . some kind of contracts . . . some kind
of waivers . . . on the dreams of the men who
dreamed

And this is definitely for the good men . . . the
good men who when knocked down . . . got up
again . . . to go just one more round . . . or show
somebody else how to do it . . . this is for the good
men who planted their dreams in the hearts of other
young men . . . this is for the good men who went
back home with their heads held high . . . who look
for ways to bend the light . . . and shine it on the
young men . . . the new dreamers . . . the talented
. . . hopeful . . . strong young men . . . who reap
the dreams . . . and plant some dreams . . . because
the best of the good men . . . are the dreams of all
men . . . so this is for Coach Reamon . . . who
talked that talk . . . and walked that walk . . . and
dreamed of change . . . this is for Coach Reamon
who knows Diamonds in the Rough are still diamonds
. . . still unusual . . . very rare . . . but always pre-
cious . . . This is definitely for holding on . . . Yeah
. . . for holding on

Nikki Giovanni
University Distinguished Professor
Virginia Tech
Blacksburg, Virginia

Rough Diamonds

Introduction

by Oliver W. Spencer Jr., Ph.D.

This powerful, compelling, and inspiring book is simply a story about a coach who refused to give up on youths who had potential but, like rough diamonds, possessed many jagged edges and needed to be cut and shaped. Furthermore, it tells the story of young men who, because of their circumstances, could have been strapped and trapped in their environment and led to believe they could not reach their dreams.

It is a true account of a caring and compassionate coach who grew up in a small rural town in Virginia. Early on in his life, he also had hopes of becoming a diamond himself, and worked toward that goal. He encountered many challenges early on in his life, and is now determined to pass on the lessons he has learned. Due to the absences of his biological father, his mother raised him and became his pillar of strength, motivation, and inspiration. These qualities would temper his desire and affect his approach to developing the lives of many young men in similar circumstances. Some of these youths have grown to be men who are now playing professional football and are providing leadership to their teams.

Noted educator Dr. Allen R. Sullivan has stated that sports have a preeminent place in the fabric of American popular culture, especially football, and it appears that most youths growing up in today's society hold professional football players in high esteem. Professional athletes can play a very significant role serving as mentors to those youths who look up to them, motivating, inspiring, and encouraging them to succeed in carrying both the ball and the books. My experience as an educator and as founder of the First and Ten Mentoring

Rough Diamonds

Program (having mentored more than 5,000 students nationwide), discussed in the last chapter of this book, gives me unique insight into these issues, and I commend this book to all educational institutions, social service agencies, libraries, coaches, and individuals who are serious about harnessing resources to provide supportive guidance and assistance to our youth. These organizations' and individuals' primary goal must be to develop rough diamonds who will shine brightly and stand out above all others.

Oliver W. Spencer Jr., Ph.D.
Educator/Consultant
Newport News, Virginia

Prologue

Atlanta Falcons Versus the New Orleans Saints, November 16, 2001: The Apex of My Coaching Career

The Falcons lost to the Saints that day.

Michael Vick of the Falcons paced the sidelines, hoping for an opportunity to play, but Coach Dan Reeves had chosen not to use him just yet. Vick experienced the same feeling as when he was a redshirt freshman at Virginia Tech, only this time as a professional quarterback. I wondered about his thoughts as he watched his opponent and cousin, Aaron Brooks of the Saints, put on a show for all of us in the Atlanta crowd. Both Vick and Brooks had to know how I beamed with pride as my most polished diamonds dazzled. Just yesterday, or so it seemed, they had spent evenings in my kitchen talking over football strategies and dreaming about the careers they were now beginning as top professionals in the National Football League.

Michael thought of Aaron as his big brother, but Aaron could be a little reserved around Michael. I thought it understandable if Aaron seemed ambivalent toward Michael; so much was happening so fast for Michael. Sure, Aaron was proud of his cousin's accomplishments, but Aaron also knew how hard he himself had worked at UVA, and often without receiving the respect he thought proper. And now that Michael was a professional, the numbers in his contract dwarfed Aaron's. I knew that had to sting just a little.

Yes, I thought, they always got along like brothers. I just hoped there wouldn't be any hard feelings on Aaron's part because of Michael's instant fame. After all, there would be a lot of pressure on Michael to live up to everyone's expectations, including his own. Aaron was luckier in a way. He had the opportunity to rise at a steadier pace. As I watched Aaron shine that afternoon, I thought about how I might explain his advantage to him, if he hadn't already thought of it himself.

I imagined Michael's thoughts as Aaron completed passes and made big plays. I was sure admiration and envy fought for Vick's mind while Brooks seized the opportunity to show his cousin what being a professional quarterback was all about. The three-year veteran and the novice professional, together. I chuckled, shaking my head over and over in disbelief as my mind wandered back over their dream seasons with me in high school and later at the University of Virginia and Virginia Tech.

A tear ran down my cheek, but I sniffled and wiped it away, hoping no one would notice. Years before, I had thought my own football career was over when my professional career ended. As all these thoughts and emotions raced through my mind, Brooks dropped back and fired a perfect spiral to an anxious, wide-open receiver downfield. He let the ball roll on his fingertips, then hauled it in underneath his right armpit and raced toward the end zone, and I momentarily relived my own runs, touchdowns, and ultimate rejection in that same NFL.

Again, I was quickly distracted from these memories by the expression of awe on Michael's face as Aaron's Saints celebrated the ensuing touchdown, dancing around their hero. As I cheered wildly amid tears of joy in the present and nostalgia for days gone by, I reminded myself that I hadn't been defeated easily. After the NFL, I had a brief Hollywood career in the television show *Kojak* and the celebrated motion picture *North Dallas Forty,* and didn't let it end there—even when my own movie project failed.

My emotions were on a roller coaster that afternoon. The pride I felt in my accomplishments as a coach seemed to do battle with the old feelings of inadequacy I experienced in my youth. In my eyes, I had been a failure in my NFL and Hollywood endeavors. I just couldn't get a firm grasp on all the opportunities that came my way. I was naïve and often trusted the judgment of others without completely forming my own.

What a strange twist of fate that I should end up here, all these years later, experiencing perfect exhilaration as a high school football coach. Why a coach? Sure, I was desperate when I came back home from Hollywood, but I remember thinking how giving something back would be a positive way to account for my failures. After all, what better way to turn failure into success than to teach others how to avoid my mistakes?

So I found, cut, and polished these diamonds, and they were on display that November day in Atlanta as fine jewelry. How did I do it? my colleagues ask. I've pondered long and hard over that question, and the only answer I can come up with is, "I let *my* dreams live on in the lives of my players." I tell them how I build personal relationships. Aaron, Michael, and all my players have become like sons. And with some modesty, I think I can say that most of them see me as a father figure. Playing that role takes a lot out of me emotionally, but look where it's gotten me.

The feelings in my heart were warm all week leading up to my trip to Atlanta. I had waited all season to see my "children" play against each other. I was interviewed by numerous television sports shows and newspapers. I rehearsed in my mind exactly how I would respond to watching my former stars play. Yet, I was nervous about every detail. This game in the Georgia Dome gave me a sense of culmination. I was finally watching them as NFL players.

That weekend in November 2001, I stayed at the Marriott Peachtree hotel near the stadium—the same hotel that Aaron Brooks stayed in when he played in the Peach Bowl for UVA. I remember sending Aaron a telegram there with good wishes in his last college football game. This was the same hotel where Virginia Tech Coach Frank Beamer stayed while Michael Vick was contemplating the decision to turn pro after having played only two years of college football. On the day of the game, as I saw the CNN Network building, I thought of the two visits their sports news crew made to Warwick High School, my school, for interviews with me about Aaron and Michael. All these memories came flooding back, reminding me of how far I'd come.

Tommy at age 12 playing in the Newsome
Park apartment complex.

1. Early Years

I was born in my grandmother's house in Halifax County, Virginia, in a country town on the Virginia/North Carolina border called Virgilinia. Virgilina is not known for much except its tobacco and corn fields. My grandmother's house was a happy place for me, and some of my earliest memories are of those days: the smell of tobacco, running in the woods, and playing with my cousins. I learned about how tobacco was grown and processed. I also learned that I hated snakes. It was a time of freedom. I reflect on those times today as my son has similar experiences when he visits with his mother in the country every other weekend. He is full of joy and fun as he plays in the woods and with the animals. Much as I did as a child, my son is able to experience both the city and country life.

I spent my early childhood years in the country, but my mother moved my family to New York City when I was five. My mother worked and went to cosmetology school. For most of my childhood, my summers would be split between New York and Halifax County as the 1960s rolled by. I have fond and sad memories of those times.

It was so crowded in New York that we played in the streets. I would see other kids hit by cars regularly. In the summertime we would play in the water that sprayed out of fire hydrants all over the streets; there wasn't a pool close to where we lived. My journeys to Yankee stadium and my dreams of playing there one day contrasted with watching the big country boys of Halifax play baseball on those country fields. Those players were so large in my eyes, and I wanted to be like them. A cousin of mine, Arthur Lee Pierce, played catcher on his baseball team.

I was so thrilled to watch Arthur throw out base runners who were attempting to steal from first to second base. He had such a strong arm, and he looked like he was having so much fun. Despite the obvious differences, the city and country athletes had one thing in common. They enjoyed life and loved what they were doing.

When I was seven, my mother, sister, brother, and I moved to Newport News, Virginia. We lived in the Newsome Park Housing Development, in the east end section of the city. It was an all-black community that consisted of low-income families. Like my mom, there were a lot of single mothers struggling to bring up fatherless children. Mom worked with a housecleaning service and had a second job as a self-employed beautician. She didn't have much of a formal education, but she had great communication skills and a personality that made everyone love her.

When I reached the age of nine, sports began to be my main focus and passion. I searched the neighborhood trying to find someone to play with. When I could, I would hang out at the playgrounds. There were not a lot of recreation facilities back in those days, and to get to the nearest school playground, I had a mile walk to the Newsome Park Elementary School. It often served as my home away from home because my mother worked long hours into the evening. My sister Willie was the baby-sitter, and watched my brother, Charles, known as C. W., and me until our mother came home from work. During these years, it seems like I was never in the house, but was always in the street.

The surprising thing was, I did not get into trouble. I was never a bored kid just seeking things to do. I was influenced by people who had the same interests that I had. My personality and behavior may have occasionally given the appearance of boredom, but I have always been a strong person who knows right from wrong. My sister Willie always said, "Tommy will kiss a ball before he'll kiss a girl." I would not totally agree with her; however, I did grow up as a very serious and focused person. I liked all sports. I played football, basketball, and baseball, and I ran track during the summers at the recreation centers.

I used to shoot hoops in a basketball goal made out of a fruit basket with a hole in the bottom nailed to the wall. Mama would get so angry with me because I was always dribbling or throwing a ball around the house. One day, she yelled at me for throwing a football through the window and breaking it. She whacked me several times with a paddle. As I stood there crying, I said to her, "But Mama, Danny told me with this ball I can go to college and one day buy us anything we want." Danny Grimes, who played football for Michigan State University in the early 1960s, was a great defensive lineman for Carver High School, and he married my cousin Edith. I always spent the weekends at their house. Danny and I would talk for hours about playing college football. After that whacking, Mama looked at me with amazement and responded by saying, "I know you will do well because you practice all the time, and Danny may be right, too. But don't you throw the ball in this house!"

I grew up without a father in the house until I was ten years old. My biological father, Paul Reamon, still lives in Newport News. He worked for the Newport News Public Schools as a custodian for many years, until he retired. I really don`t know him very well as a person. I do remember he was a heavy drinker and appeared to be a loner. I was told he left my mother when she was pregnant with me. I have never questioned my mother about what happened between her and my father. She never said one bad thing about their marriage or him, nor did I ask. I have talked with my biological father a few times through-out my life, but there has never been an effort to establish a relationship. He played no role in my life at all, except the biological one. On the other hand, my mother has been my lifelong best friend and the most solid relationship in my life. The second most important relationship in my life came about with the birth of my son, Tommy Jr.

Today I feel obligated to be helpful to my players who ask for advice on personal issues. Because of my own experience in a fatherless household, I see myself in so many of these players, and while I can't help all of them, I can assure them I will be there to listen. If a player knows his father, I encourage him to communicate with his father and try to establish some kind of relationship. In my heart, I know that this advice is given in their best interests. I encouraged Michael Vick and

Rough Diamonds

Aaron Brooks to communicate better with their fathers. Even though Michael's father was present in the home, we talked often of the tension between them. Helping Michael see the need for harmony in his family was important to me, even though I have done a poor job in my own life of dealing with an absent father.

I say this because I could have been more aggressive in pursuing the relationship. Because the absence of my father affected my life, I sought out male role models and coaches to help me in my development as a person. These people influenced me greatly—I picked up critical lessons on morals and values from them. Of course, I was unaware at the time of how much these relationships were shaping my life.

My mother got remarried when I was ten. Edward Pierce joined our family, and we moved to a new home in the southeast end of Newport News. I was proud to move into a house. At the time, the neighborhood had a mixture of white and black families, and this move was a good experience. It was my chance to meet and be exposed to white families in the neighborhood. But that did not last long, because soon after we moved there, the white families immediately began to move out of the neighborhood.

So our family grew from three children to seven. My stepfather brought in his four children, Helen, Herman, Harriet, and Homer. The house was crowded, to say the least. Even as I began to learn to get along with my new stepbrothers and -sisters, I was still in the street running behind a ball. Building new family relationships was tough on all of us as we tried to find our way and come together as a family. My mother was wonderful. She tried to be a mother to all of us. However, it appeared to be much harder for Mr. Pierce, whom I began to call my Daddy Edward, to adjust to us.

Daddy Edward was a good man. He worked at the Newport News Shipyard for forty years. He was so talented with his hands that he could build a house by himself if he had to. In my high school years he reprimanded me for not doing more chores around the house and criticized me for playing in the streets. What he didn't understand about all this "playing" was that my brother and I were pure athletes,

10

and we didn't mind putting in the time on whatever sport we played. He showed jealousy when we played sports and his children did not. Our healthy athletic interests didn't seem to matter to him.

I remember rough times in high school. We all needed to have lunch money, and he only gave it to his own children, and left it to our mother to give us ours. Many times she did not have it. I thought all this was cruel. Every morning before school, we would go into Mama and Daddy Edward's bedroom to get our lunch money, which was placed on the foot of each bedside. His children always had money on his side of the bed, and many mornings Mama's children didn't have any money on her side. So I would go without lunch money.

It got so bad that I went to one of my football coaches, Mr. Teddy Hicks, and asked him to help me with this problem. He suggested that I could be a school patrol monitor, a duty that would help keep the halls clear during lunch periods and earn me a free lunch.

The children in our family got along together because of the similarities in age. My sister Willie and Helen, Charles and Herman, and Harriet and I were all close to each other in age. Homer was the youngest. My mother and stepfather showed courage in bringing two separate families of children together as one. We all had to make the best of our situation

We all had our own dreams and goals. Throughout high school I thought I was unfairly compared with my stepsister Harriet. She was academically successful, and I was known as the jock. She was a brilliant student who studied all the time and was very disciplined. In our senior year she was class salutatorian. My teachers and classmates would tease me all the time about Harriet tutoring me or helping me with my work. She did assist me sometimes, but not often.

I remember one of my psychology teachers telling me of an incident in her class. "Harriet defended you today in class, on the topic of student athletes," she told me. A student had asked Harriet how much I studied. Harriet had replied, "Tommy simply works at whatever task lies in front of him for the moment, but perhaps not always working to his full potential. However, when he comes home at night there is little time for study. He is physically and emotionally drained, yet he manages to get assignments done as best he can." This kind of answer from a high school student showed her maturity and respect for me.

During these days and years, I was determined to make something of myself, and I knew my ticket would be playing sports. I knew that sports was my way of communicating. Sports gave me confidence in myself and attention from others. I liked feeling important, and it helped me mature as a person. I idolized many athletes that I read about and watched on television. I tried to do everything they said to do. They were my role models, representing what I wanted do with my future.

The question of whether athletes are role models is a complicated one that I am often forced to deal with when getting my players ready for college. College coaches not only want to see how my players perform on the field, they also want to know what players are like off the field. College programs do not want a player with an attitude problem or a reputation for getting into trouble. I stress to my players that what they do and say reflects on the school. Today sports and media go hand in hand. I start getting my players ready for the college and the professional level by teaching them that they must approach their sport like a business. If sports is business, then that makes today's athletes businessmen doing their jobs. They promote their product—themselves.

A few years ago "bad boy" Charles Barkley ruffled feathers by stating that he was not a role model, that it wasn't his job. Well, I say yes and no to that notion. He was right when he said that the job of role model belongs to parents. How many of us would want to give up that important job to sports stars? However, because the stars make a lot of money, children cannot help but be influenced by them. The media influences them to buy products the stars promote: shoes, sports drinks, and so on, and because of this influence, the stars do have a responsibility to be role models. They should see their role as being supportive of the parental influence, assuming that parents have done their jobs well. In short, sports stars cannot hide from the responsibility of setting the right example any more than a teacher or coach could.

My role models growing up were the men of my community, my family, my teachers, the doctor, the minister of my church, and local athletic heroes. They were conscious of how they lived their lives, what they said and did in front of kids in the neighborhood. They took responsibility not just for their own kids but for the neighbors' kids too. As a coach I know that part of my job is to set an example. In fact, it is the responsibility of every adult to be a role model to the children he or she comes into contact with. Because the sports star is an adult, he also shares in that responsibility. However, it is not his job alone. The African proverb "It takes a village to raise a child" is as true today as ever. The mass media is now part of our village, but it is up to the parents to decide how much of that media is healthy. Children who don't have healthy role models at home must receive support from the community—and shouldn't the media be included in that community?

In my eighth-grade year, I went to see the Carver High School football team play a game. I idolized a player named John Bullock, who played after the great Leroy Keyes and then followed him to Purdue University. He played running back in that game and scored three touchdowns. After the game, the team was heading to the bus, with John surrounded by fans. I was one of those fans, and I was so excited to be around him because he'd played such a great game. He had so many people coming up to him with congratulations and saying, "John, great game!" I was in awe that he responded by thanking almost every one of them. I thought to myself, "This is how you respond to people who congratulate you for doing good in a game." It may sound strange, but I really had not known how I would respond in a situation like that until I heard John. At that moment, I learned what to say to people who praised me. I learned a lesson about politeness and appreciation from modeling John's behavior.

These athletes helped me set my goals and dreams. I would always get acquainted with the local star players in high school and beg to hang out with them and play ball. Most of them were older than I was. I had an older friend named Robert Dixon, whom I just called Dixon. He played running back for the Huntington High School football team. He would tease me all the time and say, "I'm going to teach you everything I know, and then you're going to be my archrival in high school."

He lived around the corner from me, and we would spend hours and days together as I tagged along behind him to play basketball at the World War II Recreation Center. I was too small and young to play with the guys he was playing with, so I would just watch and learn from them, champing at the bit to play against them. He showed me the attitude I must possess if I wanted to be the best, and he showed me how to carry myself.

He would always tell me to get my schoolwork done so when that day came, I would be ready to play ball in high school. I listened to Dixon, and tried to go home to study and do the homework assignments, but my study habits were weak. I would start reading, but I would get distracted. Anyone could see that my attention span was short. At an early age I had problems comprehending and retaining what I had read. I was also not very good in math.

I found myself very frustrated with schoolwork. I went to summer school almost every summer to make up some failed algebra or other class or to improve my grade point average. The teachers did not give me any slack because of my athletic ability. They expected me to work as hard as the other students. I do remember the extra help the teachers gave when I asked for it, but I did not utilize the resources that I was blessed to have in high school.

Today, when my student athletes tell me that they are trying to study at home but still do badly on a quiz or test, I can relate to their frustration. I first look to their study habits. Once I hear this complaint from any player, I immediately go to his teachers, parents, and guidance counselors. I seek out help for that athlete, and come up with a plan of action. This is a must for me. It is never too early or too late. There are hundreds of great athletes who have had the potential to be college or professional players but couldn't get there because of the academic obstacles. In spite of their athletic accomplishments, many athletes are not encouraged or challenged to excel academically. The athlete's support system, which consists of parents, coaches, teachers, and their peers, must demand this success. Too many athletes appear to expect or assume that their success will be based on their athletic prowess only. I tell them that when they think like this, they are setting themselves up for a big disappointment.

One day, when Dixon and I were walking home after playing some pickup basketball games, I said, "Dixon, you and my cousin Danny keep telling me the same thing about me being too short to play college basketball."

He said, "Tommy, you've got to focus your attention and dreams on football; there are more positions to play and compete for on a team."

"I understand what you're saying. So if football is going to be my sport then I am telling you now, I will be better than Leroy Keyes."

Keyes was probably the greatest high school football player to ever play in our area. He went on to play for Purdue University after leaving Carver High School. He became an All-American and was a Heisman Trophy finalist the year O.J. Simpson won, and was drafted by the Philadelphia Eagles. Because I was a dreamer, I idolized Leroy Keyes. I did not know him very well, but I worshiped the ground he walked on. I tried to do everything that I was told by his former coaches, who became my coaches.

I had one goal, and that was to be as good as or better than Keyes. They would tell me stories of the way he practiced or performed in a given situation just to motivate me. I remember watching Keyes play in a basketball game. He wore glasses, but even with the glasses, he had this habit of squinting his eyes, as though he was having difficulty seeing. I felt this was his way of staying focused on the task at hand. I began walking around pretending that my eyes were strained. He wore the jersey number 22, and I wanted to wear anything close to him, so I got number 21.

I even attended Carver after my family moved out of its school zone. There were two high schools in my neighborhood, archrivals Huntington and Newport News, and to attend Carver, I had to travel five miles a day to school. But to follow in Keyes' footsteps, it was a small price to pay.

Rough Diamonds

As I entered Carver, I found out that I had another level of competition, against the coaches playing favorites with any athlete who lived in the North Newport News area. Keyes and some other great players came out of that part of the city, but I was living downtown. I was a very good running back, but had to prove to the coaches and the community that I could be and was the best running back who ever played at Carver High School. My experiences with the football coaches were full of mixed emotions. In early years, I had to deal with the "Keyes Mystique" and his relatives and players from his community. They were the ones chosen to excel in sports because of their connection to Keyes and the area they lived in.

They were great players, but I was too. When I tried out for the junior varsity football team, I had to beg the coach to give me a chance to try out for the running back position. I started out on the team playing center for punt snaps and linebacker on defense. One day in practice Coach John Jackson finally let me run with the football. I had waited almost half the season to finally get my hands on the ball as a running back, so I was going to make the best out of this situation. I took the handoff from the quarterback Howard Keyes, cousin of Leroy Keyes, and ran the ball to the right side of the offensive line, cut to the middle and then to the left side downfield, about forty yards, and scored. The coach said, "Tommy, you are pretty good." The remainder of the season I got better at the position, but my attitude at that time was to prove that I belonged at the running back position for the next season. The next season I played varsity and I was again center on punt snaps until one game against Union Kempsville High School. My coach, Lloyd Eason, put me in the game, and I scored my first touchdown. My teammate Ron Bullock, who played fullback, blocked a man in front of him, and I dove over him. After the touchdown, Ron said, "Tommy, I thought you were going to go crazy after you scored." I said, "Ron, you haven't seen anything yet, just wait until next year." I promised to myself that the best was yet to come.

I talk about these experiences to my players, because it is so important for them to understand that only hard-won efforts feed the

Senior year at Carver High. Tommy is team co-captain number 21 at the coin toss against Ferguson High at Todd Stadium.

desire to excel, and make it even stronger. These are the true self-esteem builders.

I was not very fast when I entered high school, and I had to learn various techniques in running to improve my speed. A former running back from Carver, named Vernon Lee, was home for summer vacation from Virginia State College. I went to him and asked him to help me improve my speed and show me some basic techniques used by running backs.

These instructions became critical to me as I saw improvements. The greatest lesson I learned was that you have to work on weaknesses. My coaches always used to say, "Work on weaknesses; your strengths will take care of themselves." That made sense to me then, and it still does. Along that line of thinking, I also believed another of my coaches' sayings, "Hard work will beat talent if talent isn't trained." A person with desire will be more willing to work on weaknesses, and ultimately become more successful.

I started reading about football camps being held around the state, featuring college and professional football players. These players would come to the camp to work on football techniques in an atmosphere of fun and fellowship. I wanted to attend so badly, but could not afford to go. I promised myself that if I ever made it big one day, I would have my own football camp to help youths who could not afford to attend a camp.

My senior year came upon me too fast. I was an average student attempting to prepare myself academically and athletically to go to college, and was able to do what was necessary to stay above water. My grades had improved to the point that there were some colleges, mainly predominantly black institutions, that would admit me. However, I wanted to play at a major university—and to play on television. When the bigger schools started contacting me, the first thing they wanted to know was my grade point average and SAT scores. I had to score 800 on the SATs to qualify for an athletic scholarship.

I took the test three times, and the highest score I got was 720. My guidance counselor, Mrs. Floria Crittenden, now a member of the House of Delegates for the state of Virginia, tutored me on both the math and verbal sections of the test. Mama Crittenden, as I call her, fussed at me for years to get my grades. She counseled me during this difficult time, and wrote the following in my senior yearbook:

> Tommy, you could have been a better than average student, but you were not challenged to do so. Motivation and nurturing the value of education are

important to success and both were lacking in your educational experience. I hope you will find this success in junior college, before you transfer to the University of Missouri.

Tommy's senior yearbook portrait.

I attended a junior college because I wanted to play in a major football program, and I dreamed of being on television. Because of these ambitions I even turned down a full scholarship to Norfolk State University. My low grade point average and SAT scores kept me out of consideration for a major university program unless I first went to a junior college. I chose Fort Scott Community College in Kansas because they had a football program, and many junior colleges in Virginia did not have football programs in those days.

2. Junior College

In 1970, I boarded a plane and headed for Fort Scott Community College in Kansas. The first leg of the trip took me to Kansas City, Missouri. On the plane, I could not keep from crying a little bit. This was my first time away from home, heading to a new and different place where there wouldn't be anyone who knew me or anyone I knew. I felt a real fear of what prejudices I might be facing in Kansas because of my experiences in the South. Growing up, I'd had very little contact with Whites socially, and now here I was going to an almost all-white environment because of a dream to play big-time college football. I questioned my decision many times on the flight.

Fort Scott is about 70 miles southeast of Kansas City. Dick Foster, the head football coach, and his brother Bill, who lived in Kansas City, met me at the airport to drive me down to Fort Scott.

It looked so much like the Old West, I thought that when I landed I would see cowboys and Indians. I didn't, but what I did see was miles and miles of treeless land with cattle and other farm animals. The vastness and emptiness of the land was startling. It was so spread out that in my imagination, I could have brought the overpopulated city of New York and placed it there and had room to spare. Fort Scott, Kansas, is known for its historical military fort used during the Mexican War. We entered the town and traveled straight down its main street to the school, located at the opposite end of town. I asked Coach Foster if we had gone through the entire town. He said we had, and in a blink of an eye we were back in the empty, flat landscape.

We approached a small brick building with the name Fort Scott Community College on it. The building was no larger than my high school. There was no football field in view. "Coach, where do we play our football games?" I asked.

He said we would use the Fort Scott High School football field. I noticed some horse stables and cattle bends not far from the practice field. I asked Coach Foster about these animals, and he said the college had one of the top rodeo programs in the country. I could only think about how this small town, and this strange school with a great rodeo program but no football field, located nearly 2,000 miles away from home, would be the place that I would spend the next two years of my life.

The first few days set the tone for what would be an experience to remember. I stayed with six other players in a big house a few blocks from campus. There were no dormitories. The first morning, we had a team meeting. I was so excited to meet the players and see my competition for the starting running back position. I was stunned to see so many white players. I had come from an all-black high school, and I had never played with any white players.

There were about twelve black players, and ten of us were from out of state. The interesting thing was we all played the same skill positions—a lot of running backs, defensive ends, linebackers, and receivers. The coaches recruited the out-of-state players for these positions because they had speed and quickness. The linemen and quarterbacks were all in-state white players. The Kansas junior colleges had a rule that each school could have only ten out-of-state players, and the coaches told me before I came there that the best ten players would make the team. I was not afraid that I would not make the team, but I could see, for the first time, that football was a brutal business. The best players from out of state competed for those ten spots on the team and a scholarship that paid for tuition and books only. The black players from out of state each came to junior college because of grade problems, whereas the majority of white players were better students. Each player had his own reasons to attend a junior college, but the one thing we all shared was the need to prove something, whether it was to improve our football talents or to earn a scholarship or placement in a four-year college.

My roommate, Hosie Moss, was a huge fullback from Poplar Buff, Missouri. He was a high school All American and had been voted the best high school football player in the state of Missouri. However, we shared the same problem: coming out of high school with low grade point averages and SAT scores. The first night in our house, many of the players came into our room to talk. There was no curfew, so we talked all night about our homes, the reasons we came to junior college, and our dreams and goals for the future.

The first day, we were scheduled to practice three times. The first practice in the morning, I was so nervous because I worried about my talents compared with those of the other running backs. During an individual running back drill, I watched the other players try to perform some fundamental techniques such as stance, steps, form running with the ball, and handoffs from the quarterback. The objective was to demonstrate their quickness to get the ball and how fast they could return to the line of scrimmage. During this drill, my confidence, and what some people at home called arrogance, took over the nervousness I had. I knew that I was better fundamentally and had been better coached.

By the second practice, I was lined up as the first team running back, and my roommate, Hosie, was the fullback. During a no-pads blocking drill, Hosie and I were working together. He accidentally hit me in the mouth and split my bottom lip. I refused to leave practice to see if the cut required stitches. After the incident I remember saying to myself, "I hope I don't ever have to tackle him."

During the third practice, Hosie began to have cramps all over his body. The coach left with Hosie in an ambulance to take him to the hospital. That night, he did not return to the room. I was scared to death because I did not know what was wrong with him. Just the night before, we had sat up in our beds and talked all night. The next morning in the locker room, before the coaches could assemble us, I spoke with Coach Foster. I remember he had on sunglasses, and I thought that was strange. He said, "Tommy, Hosie died." I was shocked. I couldn't believe someone my own age could just die like that. I began to cry. I told Coach Foster that I could not stay.

Hosie's death was devastating to me, but Coach Foster helped me through it with compassion. He asked me if there was anything he could do for me. I said I missed my family, and now the friend I had made was gone. I asked to stay at his house for a few days, and he welcomed me. The doctor's report on the cause of Hosie's death was that he had sickle cell anemia and died during a crisis. I tried to stay focused on my reason for being there, but I was very homesick.

One night two weeks later, Matthew Brown, another of my roommates, who lived in the upstairs bedroom above me, was sleepwalking and went through a plate-glass window and fell from his second-story bedroom. His arm required more than a hundred stitches. The next morning I went to Coach Foster and said, "Coach I have had enough. I am going home."

I called my mother, thinking she would say to come on home, but she surprised me. She said, "You are not leaving because things are tough—you decided to go out there, so you have to be strong enough to finish what you started."

I realized she was right. I could not leave simply because I could not have faced the people who questioned my decision to turn down a signed football scholarship to the predominately black Norfolk State University. I decided first to attend a junior college in hopes of being eligible to play at a major college.

A close relationship began between myself and Coach Foster and his wife Karen. Coach Foster sensed my need for family. I had not been around many white people before, except in my junior year in high school, when the integration movement was just getting started. Two white coaches, John Finfroak and Gary Silvey, had joined our football staff. Today Coach Silvey is the athletic director of the Newport News Public Schools, in which I am one of his head football coaches. Because my experience with white coaches was minimal, Coach Foster always talked to me about how not to look at a person's skin color or where they came from but what type of person they were on and off the field.

Once school and the games started, I made the adjustment and felt more comfortable each day. I spent a lot of time with three men: Bob

Shores, our defensive coordinator; Jim Hammer, an insurance salesman and an alumnus of the University of Missouri; and Coach Cowdrey, the recruiting coach at Missouri, who was responsible for getting me to Fort Scott. They would spend countless hours talking with me about the adjustments I had to make in this new environment. They were my role models during those days. They worked together to get me adjusted to college life, football, and being away from home.

Coach Shores always said, "Tommy, you're able to survive these first few weeks because of an inner drive to be the best football player to come out of the Newport News area and to continue on to play at a major college."

I declared after Hosie's death that I would play football for the both of our dreams. Coach Foster picked me as the starting running back, and while I adjusted to academic life, I also found myself eating and sleeping football. I had gone to junior college to better my academics and play football, and those were the only two things I did. The low pupil-to-teacher ratio provided an excellent classroom setting for instructional learning. The individual attention on course work helped me to learn, and I could work on the study habits that I never took responsibility for in high school. However, school and football were not the only benefits I enjoyed.

I also learned a great deal about people and relationships. The people of this small town and school environment helped influence my life forever, including how I coach. They gave me confidence; they helped me to develop a caring attitude and appreciation of people. The coaches were experts at helping players adjust to the culture shock of coming from the city life to a small town. They would regularly invite me and other players to their homes for dinner, and actually opened their homes to us to sleep over or visit all evening. I used to wonder where they got the heart to do these special things to help us adjust to being away from home. Little did I know at the time how much it would influence the way I treat my own players.

Not only did the coaches take a personal interest in us, but our teammates from Kansas would invite us to their homes for the weekend or on the holidays. Their families were just as enthusiastic as their children, and made sure we enjoyed our visits. I remember after every football game, either the evening of the game or next morning, I would go to my door and open it to find desserts or food gifts lying on the steps. Their generosity extended to everyone on campus, so it wasn't just because we played football. I always tell my players today that people do not have to do anything for you. When they do, appreciate what they say or do, and *show* them that you appreciate it, rather then expecting favors. I tell them to be humble and be appreciative of their talents, and they will be well rewarded in life.

During my junior college career I played in the National Junior College Championship game two consecutive years. We were the national champions in 1971 and national runner-up in 1972. The Shrine Bowl was probably the best game of my junior college career. My mother flew down to the game in Savannah, Georgia. I broke three records and tied one. On the first play of the game, quarterback Kurt Neiman pitched the ball to me and I went 68 yards, which was a record. I had 234 yards rushing on 29 carries and 3 touchdowns to win the game and the national title. I was the only freshman selected first team All-American, and I led the nation in touchdowns, in total offense in receiving and rushing yards, and in rushing with 1,816 yards on 253 carries. I became the only player in NJCAA history to be named two times national offensive player of the year.

On November 15, 1971, the *Gridiron* newspaper sent writer Phil Henzel to interview me before our second national championship game appearance held again in Savannah, Georgia. The story was entitled, "Heroes, Tomorrow's . . . Tommy Reamon: 'This year, I'm running for mercy!'" Henzel said of me:

He just might be the best junior college player in the country. He is one of the most sought after players. He flatly admits, "I've been contacted by every conference in the nation." He's that good! Fort Scott's football coach Walt Olinger declares, "Reamon is the greatest back I've ever seen." And as far as comparisons with O.J. Simpson or any other backs—look at the records!" Reamon is an individual to the extent that he tends to be a loner and often will leave a crowd to be alone with his thoughts. At most sports events, he may go to the game with friends, but before long will be sitting by himself—leading one to believe that even though Tommy is just watching, he doesn't want to have his thoughts interrupted.

I was named to the NJCAA all-time best offensive backfield in its first fifty years. The other backs were O.J. Simpson and Terry Metcalf. In1997, I was selected and inducted to the NJCAA hall of fame. I am the only player from Fort Scott Junior College to have been given this honor.

The recruiting process for deciding what university I would transfer to for my remaining two years was fascinating, and some people would say Tommy Reamon changed the NCAA rules. I was recruited legally and illegally, and visited over fifteen colleges throughout a two-year period. The under-the-table offers of cash and cars were eye-popping. I found out how businesslike some of these schools could be. I could write a book just on the seduction of a teenage student athlete by college coaches. I use this experience to help my players and their parents during their decision-making time. Even though many of the NCAA rules have changed for the better, the race to recruit the best players still continues.

I remember visiting one major college football program. They flew me from Newport News, where I was at home for the Thanksgiving weekend, and I had to get back to school after the break. I decided to visit their campus on the way back, even though the students were not on campus. I was picked up at the airport by one of the coaches, and we drove up to the hotel I was staying in. I looked up at the marquee of the hotel, where the words were spelled out, "The university welcomes Tommy Reamon."

We got out of the car and walked into the hotel lobby. I saw the recruiting coach, and we shook hands. In that handshake, the coach had just handed me a hundred-dollar bill. We got up the next morning to visit the football stadium. I had never in my life seen true bluegrass on a football field.

We then drove up to a brick business building, and the coach said, "Tommy, you are going to meet one of our top football boosters." We entered his office and I was introduced. He began to tell me, "Tommy we really want you here very badly. We know you are close to your mother and girlfriend. If you come here, they will be able to attend every home game. They will be flown here from Newport News in one of our company airplanes. We want to give you one thousand dollars at the signing of the letter of intent and then an additional fifteen hundred dollars upon signing the national letter of intent." (In those days a student athlete had to sign two letters of intent.)

He continued, "We will give you a clothes allowance of five hundred dollars and an automobile to drive."

I was only nineteen years old, and here I was in an office being sought after to play football by a well-respected businessman. The offer was wonderful. I was sitting there thinking that I needed that money badly. I was tempted. However, I was proud of myself that I did not take the deal. I told the coaches that I would think over their offer and let them know. They flew me on to school, and this saved me the cost of a plane ticket. I felt honored to have this college so interested in my talents. It was a big boost to my self-confidence.

I decided to visit as many colleges as I could because I wanted to travel and see the country. Because I had not met the NCAA requirements for a student athletic scholarship coming out of high school, I felt that I had the opportunity in junior college to experience the college recruiting process as a top football recruit. Today I tell my players to experience the college recruiting process and enjoy the five official visits that are allowed under the NCAA rules.

When I decided to visit both UCLA and the University of Southern California, I had my own plan to travel and enjoy the recruiting process for all it was worth. I told USC that I wanted to be recruited by O.J. Simpson, who was an alumnus. They agreed to that request, and I decided to visit their school. The coaches had arranged for me to meet with him, and we had breakfast together with his son Jason and longtime friend and teammate, Al Cowans.

I was excited to meet O.J., and we talked about my high school idol and hometown boy Leroy Keyes. He and Keyes had been the finalists for the Heisman Trophy in the same year. As players, O.J. and Keyes were very important, and to me, being recruited by O.J. Simpson was the next-best thing to being recruited by Leroy Keyes. It also helped relieve some old feelings of doubt that I had carried on my shoulders for years. If the University of Southern California thought enough of my talents to have O.J. Simpson recruit me, then they must have thought that I was on the same level as O.J. Simpson and the man who was still my hero, Leroy Keyes.

I had my picture taken with O.J. at a breakfast meeting that morning. He told me he decided to attend USC because he was so well known in California. I took him to mean that if I was so well known in the Midwest and had made a name for myself in junior college, then why not go to a school in the Midwest? I met O.J. Simpson many more times over the years as a player and then as an actor in Los Angeles. That picture we took together at breakfast would come to mind some twenty-five years later, as I watched him on national television.

It was the famous telecast of the Bronco chase, before his murder trial. The chase ended at his mansion as Jason ran out of the front door and approached the driver's side door to talk with O.J. and Al Cowans. As I witnessed that scene, I visualized us four together at the breakfast table, on my junior college trip to Los Angeles.

I also remembered that O.J. had introduced me to Nicole one July Fourth, at their home, where they were having a large picnic. She impressed me as a warm and caring person. At the time, I was most excited about meeting Marcus Allen, who had just graduated from USC. During the weeks following the Bronco chase, his name and involvement with the family would come up again and again.

Not long after that picnic O.J. and I had sat together on a plane trip to Los Angeles from San Francisco. At first we discussed our careers and football. I told him that I had idolized him while I was in high school, even though he had been competing against my hometown hero Leroy Keyes for the Heisman trophy. Gradually our conversation turned more personal, involving our families and mutual friends. He spoke about his divorce and the criticism he was getting from the Black community for leaving his black wife and then dating and marrying a white woman. He said his critics didn't understand what it was like to grow up Black in America, then experience great success and, at the same time, be introduced to the glamorous lifestyle that goes along with it. Meanwhile, back home, his black wife did not understand the world he was now living in, and when he tried to expose her to that world, she did not feel comfortable in it. Because his wife, Marguerite, did not grow in the same direction, problems started.

He confided that he enjoyed his new social life, but she did not. Eventually they went from fighting about his social life to fighting about

Tommy (center) at breakfast with O.J. Simpson. Al Cowlings at left and Jason Simpson in foreground.

everything. I remember O.J. saying, "Black women's personalities are just so strong—She can't just be Mrs. O.J. Simpson and be happy. She just wants to fight about everything all the time." He went on to describe how intolerable their situation had become. On the other hand, he said he enjoyed white women because they were more "worldly and intelligent." Because they found him fascinating, it made him feel special. He imagined that any one of them would be happy to be "Mrs. O.J." He said that white women just don't have all the hang-ups that black women do. He further imagined that with white women, he could enjoy a stress-free relationship without the hassles he had been experiencing.

Now, here I sat watching him get arrested for the murder of his white wife, a woman with whom his relationship had reportedly been filled with violence and turmoil. After knowing O.J., the tragedy and irony of that moment were terrible for me.

On that same visit to the West Coast, I had an illegal visit to UCLA's campus. I was to go to the airport as if I were leaving from USC. However, I was not to board the plane. Instead, I was to meet the coach from UCLA at the boarding gate. I then enjoyed two more days in Los Angeles.

On my next recruiting trip, I traveled to Texas Tech University in Lubbock, Texas. The first-class treatment demonstrated by their coaching staff started as the airplane rolled toward the gate. As I was exiting the airplane, the airline stewardess said to me, "You must be very important." I looked at her, wondering what she was talking about. Suddenly, as I turned my head to step down off the plane, I saw a red carpet walkway leading toward a long black limousine. I remember saying to the stewardess as I exited the plane, "I think I feel like the President." In May 2001, I saw the recruiting coach, who had recruited me during this visit to Texas Tech. We laughed about the great treatment I had been given then. However, he quickly noted that players today would not be treated that way, in fear of violating NCAA rules.

My final recruiting trip would take me to the University of Texas, El Paso. It was my hometown friend Lonnie Crittenden who had convinced me to visit their campus. Lonnie is the son of Mama Crittenden, my high school guidance counselor. While there, I would visit Juarez, Mexico, and eat a 64-ounce steak. Today when I tell this story nobody believes I could have eaten a steak that large; even I have difficulty believing it.

I returned to Fort Scott and met with an attorney, who had been recommended by another hometown friend, Bennie McRae, a former defensive back in the 1960s with the Chicago Bears. They had convinced me to challenge the NFL rule that prohibited a player from entering the NFL until his four years of college were completed. I felt that I was good enough to play professionally. The attorney met with a friend of Bennie's named Buddy Young, who worked for the NFL's league office. I was mentally prepared to do whatever they decided was in my best interest.

After weeks of contemplating the decision to petition the NFL, I became very discouraged. A lawsuit would be the only recourse. I was afraid that I would lose; therefore, I decided to sign with the University of Missouri.

In 2000, when Michael Vick was entertaining the idea of entering the NFL draft, I had mixed emotions about whether he should remain in school and complete his education or whether he should enter the NFL draft. The teacher in me wanted him to complete his education because Michael was a role model for many kids in the community. A decision by him to remain in school would serve as a positive example and show the importance of an education. However, the athlete in me understood his decision to forgo his last two years of college football.

In 1998, I was inducted into the National Junior College Athletic Association Hall of Fame. A ceremony was held at Fort Scott Community College in Fort Scott, Kansas, and my former head coach, Dick Foster, presented the following speech:

> In Tommy's freshman year, he was selected first team All-American, scored 23 touchdowns, 138 points, and led the nation not only in scoring, but rushing with 1,582 yards on 224 carries. He had great quickness, vision, and running ability, but more importantly, he had the inner drive to be the best player on the field. The bigger the game, the better he played. Tommy had great confidence in his abilities, regardless of how tough the situation was. He liked to compete and was not afraid of the players you had in

your program because he knew he could beat anyone out as long as you gave him a chance. You could tell he had great teachers and childhood role models. He showed much respect for his coaches, teachers, and fans. It was always "Mr. or Mrs. Foster." There is no question that the strong feeling he has for respect was developed in him at an early age by his mother.

The relationship he had with his high school coaches, myself, Coach Charlie Cowdrey, and Jack Pardee developed his understanding of the importance of a player/coach relationship. He knew how important it was in his development and he has carried it over to his association with the players he is coaching today.

TO: MARLENE "My LOVE"
FROM: TOMMY

3. University of Missouri

When I decided to attend the University of Missouri, I had great expectations. Upon signing the scholarship papers, I just knew that I had made the right decision. The signing day was at my home in Newport News. The Missouri coaches flew there in a private airplane that belonged to Mr. Robert Baskowitz from St. Louis, Missouri, home of the famous Budweiser beer company. This day is so clear in my mind because the Anheuser-Busch brewery was about to open for business in Williamsburg, Virginia. I visited the brewery with the coaches and Melvin Price, a local Budweiser distributor from Hampton, Virginia. The red carpet was rolled out for me just like the entire recruiting process to sign me for my services as a football player.

The visit to the brewery was political because Mr. Baskowitz and the coaches had promised to help me get a summer job. Mr. Baskowitz, known by everyone as Mr. B., was a true booster. He supported the football program wholeheartedly—although, to tell the truth, I never asked if he had ever attended the University of Missouri. I only knew the story that his father had been in the military service with Mr. Busch, the owner of Budweiser, and the two of them had agreed to start a business, with Mr. Baskowitz's father furnishing the bottles and, naturally, Mr. Busch supplying the beer.

The media had publicized my coming to Missouri as the savior of a team that had dropped in stature in the powerful Big Eight Conference. The media made a big deal out of Missouri signing the best junior college player in the country, and focused its attention on my decision to attend a college that had a 1-10 win-loss record the previous year. Many questions would prompt an inquiry by the NCAA into possible recruiting violations by Missouri. Kansas State University's head football coach, Vince Gibson, stated in a newspaper article that I should have been investigated for possible NCAA wrongdoing. There were many rumors about my recruiting process. The interesting thought I had when I heard this was that Kansas State and Kansas University were two schools that I visited more than three times. The recruiting rivalry between those two schools and Missouri was furious. I personally feel that these schools were jealous of my decision, and one, if not both, contacted the NCAA to say that Missouri and I must have violated some rules in order to sign me.

I would like to set the record straight, even if it is thirty years after the fact. There was no wrongdoing by either of us. I was not given anything improper, nor did I accept any money or a car. The rumors stopped as soon as I arrived at the University of Missouri preseason football practice. I was now ready to take on the challenge of helping Missouri rise to the top of football powers.

The media was the first to set the tone of high expectations for me, and I felt the pressure a bit too much. Prior to the football season, the Big Eight Conference sportswriters toured each conference school and interviewed players and coaches. They called this "press day." However, I declined to talk with the press. I felt there was nothing else to say. I had not yet played a down of football for Missouri. I was tired of the publicity I was getting, and I was having difficulty in summer practice adjusting to my new role as a "wishbone" running back. I was working as hard as I could; I felt that the talking was over and it was time to show what kind of football player I was.

It was a big mistake not to talk to the sportswriters on press day. This was the first time I had experienced a negative reaction from the press. The reports insinuated that because I didn't talk during the session, I was unhappy with Missouri and I had retreated into a shell. It came across like I was dissatisfied on the second team. That was true, but I understood I had to work myself into the starting lineup.

I was trying to get used to an offensive formation called the wishbone, and would be on second team for a while until I proved myself at it. The formation consisted of three backs positioned behind the quarterback. The fullback is positioned two yards directly behind the quarterback, with two halfbacks lined up behind the offensive tackles and beside the fullback. I didn't like this formation, mainly because it kept me from getting my hands on the ball as much as I wanted. I was trying to learn how to block and get accustomed to the coaches' expectations of me in this new environment, and all the while I was a little bit resentful that I wasn't getting the ball.

My teammates had had the opportunity to learn the new offensive system in spring practice, so I never questioned the reserve role going into our first game of the season. I was not confident with the new offense, and I thought it would be best to wait and play when I had that confidence. I even told a reporter from the Columbia *Missourian* later, "The way I was looking at it, I shouldn't start the first game." However, I did play in our opening-game win over Oregon, and was the leading rusher.

The preseason press fiasco was the first roadblock for me. The second, and more important, was a rash of fumbles that plagued me in the early season. I had never fumbled like that before, and I felt that lack of playing time and not carrying the football enough were at the root of it. However, I did not let myself get psyched out as some runners do when something like this strikes, and soon was able to hang on to the ball. But then I broke my left hand while blocking a defensive linebacker, which just added to my fear of fumbling the football. It also caused me to be a bit timid in my performances for next three games, as I had to learn how to use my right hand to carry the football when running to the left. As the hand healed, I could feel more confidence in my performances, and I played very well in our upset wins against the previously undefeated Notre Dame and Colorado teams. Yet I was not satisfied. I felt I needed to carry the ball more, about twenty times per game, and I was candid about my distaste for the wishbone offense. I had known before signing that they were going to play this offense some, but I didn't know they were going to run it so much.

The decision to go to Missouri and play in that wishbone offense haunted me at every practice and during games throughout that first season. I learned a lot about myself during that time of frustration. I became convinced that the coaches had lied to me during the recruiting process. They knew that I wanted to play in the I-formation, where the running back runs with the football—I had made that such a issue in the recruiting process. I could only conclude that they did not care what I wanted as a person. They were looking at it as a business.

Today I draw upon this knowledge, and request that my players' parents let me be involved with their college recruiting process, but to be fair, I stay out of their final decisions. I help the players investigate the colleges they are interested in and meet with the recruiting coaches. I must have a feeling of trust toward the receiving coach. I will ask him to show me how he plans to utilize my player's talents in his program, and he should be able to communicate his plan for my player. If he can't tell me his plan, and if I don't get that sense of trust, I advise my player to look elsewhere.

My personal expectations during the first football season at Missouri were not realized. The overall team performance was great, but we were inconsistent throughout the season. It was unusual that we played well enough to upset the undefeated Notre Dame in South Bend and again at the University of Colorado in the same year. I always bring up these games to my players today when we prepare for a big game, and talk to them about how they should prepare themselves mentally and physically. At Missouri, being the underdog motivated us to excel, and that's what I tell my players when they start thinking too highly of themselves and their skills.

Before the Notre Dame game, an article appeared in *Sports Illustrated* that quoted me as saying, "If Missouri plays me in the I-formation backfield set, and if I carry the football twenty times, we will win." I certainly showed some arrogance and frustration by making this kind of statement to the press. However, I believed in myself and I was helpless in getting the coaches to treat me fairly by recognizing that my talents were not being utilized. I truly believed that if I *did* carry the football more—if they would just take advantage of what I had to offer—we would win. The media ate it up. They talked about my comments for weeks and the coaches did not like that. As a result, I created a lot of tension. I did not realize that the coaches would take my comments as a criticism of their coaching and of their system, and I now believe that I handled this situation poorly. Coach Onofrio called me into his office to talk with me about my comments, and we compromised. I agreed that I should not say any more about the offense, and he agreed to use me a little more in the I-formation.

I relived this experience in Aaron Brooks' junior year at the University of Virginia, in which he began the season as the starting quarterback. The year before, he had shared playing time with another quarterback named Tom Sherman, the son of an assistant coach on the staff. Brooks was the better player and had proved it on the field; however, he had lost valuable playing experience that year, and his talents were not utilized to the fullest. As the new season started, Brooks was learning from a new offensive coach, and the team had some pretty tough losses. Because he was the quarterback, the blame fell right on him, and he was unfairly criticized by the press. Brooks was frustrated about the criticism and began to use the media to get his message out. We talked one evening after a game at which the sports writers had asked him some tough questions. I said to him, "Be careful about how you answer some of those questions."

"Coach, if they had not wasted my time last season and played me, I wouldn't be going through this, and I would be on the top of my game," he said, his frustration showing.

I agreed. "Yeah, I know, but you can't show them emotions. Keep your head up. The press will not only write what you say but some things you didn't say."

I had long talks with him about how to handle the press, the backlash he could get from the coaches, about not using the press to make a statement in front of them. This would be bad on his relationships with them and the situation altogether.

I did a lot of soul-searching to get through the rest of that season at Missouri. I was taking two elective classes on the Bible, which I have always thought helped me. I have never been a very religious person in a traditional sense, but I have strong feelings of spirit and faith in God Almighty. I was using all my resources to get through my disappointment at Missouri. When I registered for classes that first year, I had been excited to pursue a physical education major. My junior college experience with coaches helped me make the decision that I wanted to be a high school coach. However, by my junior year, my faith in the player/coach relationship that I had once believed to be a key ingredient in my early success was being shattered, and I no longer wanted to coach.

I had come to Missouri with a lot of publicity and promise, but the coaches did not know how to help me adjust to the real-life issues and experiences I found there. I had genuine concerns about my playing time, talents being utilized, and making personal adjustments as a student, but the coaches' lack of communication skills with these kind of issues turned me off so much that I did not want to pursue a coaching career.

Today, I tell my players the real deal. I tell them the truth about important issues like whether or not they can play, if they have the talent to compete for a position, or if they can play college football. I tell them the truth, regardless of how much it hurts their feelings or dreams. I feel they must learn how to deal with or adjust to adversities. I relate my experiences to them, so that they will have no illusions, and will be prepared for the real-life experiences and politicking they could experience. The Missouri coaches were good people, but they had a job to do, and my dreams at times were not important to them. The one coach for whom I had a lot of respect as a man was Prentice Gautt. He was the first black player to play at the University of Oklahoma. I would talk with him often and he would give me good sound advice, but he could not make things happen or influence the coaches who were unfair.

I prayed all the time in those days, asking the Lord to help me deal with the disappointments in my game performances and my feeling that I wasn't getting the chance I deserved. I remember a homecoming game against Oklahoma State University. My mother, stepfather and high school girlfriend came to see me play. I had two fumbles in that game. The fans booed me, and the coach took me out of the game. The next week I started carrying a football tucked under my arms as I walked around campus, to practice the correct way to hold on to it. I looked so stupid, but the purpose was to concentrate on carrying the ball. I had many people laughing at me, and a few stopped me to ask what I was doing. Today, when one of my running backs is having problems holding on to the football, I have him take the ball home and bring it back the next day and carry it throughout the day at school.

Even though I struggled to find an answer to my problems at Missouri, the one thing that stayed with me was my confidence in myself. In the last game of the season, we played Arizona State in the second annual Fiesta Bowl, and the truth came to the surface. In the

Tommy, number 21 again, sprinting downfield against Iowa State.

Fiesta Bowl, we ran out of the I-formation, and I rushed for 150-plus yards and a touchdown. However, we still lost the game—but my performance in that bowl game set the tone for my last year at Missouri. In my senior year, I led the team in rushing and returned the team to its second straight bowl game. In the Sun Bowl in El Paso, Texas, I rushed for 120-plus yards against Auburn, and we won. After the game, I spoke to Mr. Baskowitz, the team's booster and Anheuser-Busch businessman. He teased me, saying, "Tommy, I always know when you will have a great game."

"What do mean, Mr. B?"

"Whenever we play on national television or the camera's rolling, you play your best! Tommy, if you ever need something, let me know. Don't forget I helped take care of you. Don't forget that."

I remember saying, "Mr. B, I won't forget you, and I will call you."

When my two seasons at Missouri were over, the deep bitterness I felt about how my talents were not utilized would ultimately carry me into the world of professional football and the decision that would lengthen or shorten my career.

The one thing I say about my experience at Missouri, and it helps my players today, is that you do not have to travel 2,000 miles away from home to get a good education and play football. The TV exposure and the chance for the NFL to see you can happen at any school. Even though I spent a lot of lonely hours and days by myself out in the Midwest, the Missouri experience taught me some inner toughness that I carried with me for many years. I had taken my dreams into this school, and many were shattered, but I managed to adjust mentally and find a way to be happy and content while serving my time.

4. Early Pro Years

One day after a workout at the Missouri field house complex, I went up to the coaches' offices to use the telephone. I heard a projector on in the film meeting room. I walked into the dark room but could not see anyone in there. I sat down in the front row of seats and began to watch the film that was being played. Suddenly, I heard a voice I didn't recognize.

The man asked me, "Are you Tommy Reamon?"

"Yes."

"How do you think your career has gone here at Missouri?"

"It could have been better."

He immediately commented, "You had a real good year. I have followed you since you played in junior college."

"Thank you, and who are you?"

He said, "I work for the Pittsburgh Steelers."

I got nervous, and before I could say anything else to him, the lights came on and one of the coaches walked into the room.

I said to the scout, "It was nice meeting you, sir," then left the room.

After the football season at Missouri, I was determined to be ready both mentally and physically if the NFL scouts came to campus. I started training sessions twice a day—distance running in the morning and weightlifting and sprint workouts in the afternoon. I lived on a diet of tuna fish, "nature's perfect food," to keep me lean. I was anxious to find out if I would have a professional career. I had my last opportunity to be with my teammates on the night of the annual football awards. I had no desire to attend, and I decided to drive down to St. Louis and stay in a hotel. I told the coaches I had to go out of town. I could not face them again.

Rough Diamonds

When I returned to Columbia that Monday, I attended a ceremony where the coaches gave me the Most Outstanding Offensive Back award. I accepted it, and although I was very grateful for the honor, I could only think of all the dreams and goals I had when I chose to come to Missouri that were never fulfilled. As I looked at the award, I couldn't help but think that if only my talents had been better used, I would be earning bigger awards, and I would know how I stood in the eyes of the professional football scouts. As I walked away from the athletic complex, I looked over toward the football field. I paused for a minute or two, gazing at the empty stadium. I reminisced over the great plays that had led to the award which now closed my relationship with Missouri. My heart was heavy over the missed opportunities. However, I was more concerned about the opportunity to turn pro than I was about getting my degree. My thinking was that I could always go back and get the degree later, or even during the off-season.

On the day of the NFL draft, I did what all players do. I sat by the telephone. I didn't want to talk to or be around anyone. I did not get The Call that first day. I had dreamed that playing at Missouri would give me a chance at being a number-one draft choice. I knew what I was capable of doing. I just needed the chance to show it. Missouri was to have been my chance, but now I could only sit by the phone and wonder if I would get my shot at the NFL. I had already been contacted by several agents. One agent in Kansas City actually brought me the first birthday cake I ever had on my twenty-first birthday. However, I did not sign with him or any of the others.

Today, when my athletes are going through lonely moments waiting by the phone on those draft days, my heart waits with them. I relive each of those painful moments waiting for "The Call," the one on which all your dreams and hopes depend. When Kwamie Lassiter, now an eight-year NFL veteran with the Arizona Cardinals, Aaron Brooks, Michael Vick, and others I have coached talk about the recruiting process, I can identify with them about the pitfalls and disappointments from my own experiences.

On the second day of the NFL draft, I got The Call. I remember the exact moment; the radio was on, playing the O'Jays' "For the Love of Money" just as I answered the phone. The Pittsburgh Steelers had drafted me, and I jumped for joy. I was selected as their ninth player in a class of players that would be known as the Super Bowl draft class that changed the Steelers' organization. Some of the top choices were Lynn Swann, Lynn Stallworth, Jack Lambert, Mike Webster, and Donnie Shell. As impressive as it might sound to hear my name on this list, I was still a low draft choice.

The next day I also got a call from the newly formed World Football League. The team that selected me was originally in Norfolk, Virginia, but then moved to Orlando, Florida, where they became the Blazers. The player personnel director was named Dwayne Jeter, a former head coach at the black college, Virginia State University. Sixteen years later, he would be an assistant principal at Manor High School in Portsmouth, Virginia, where I landed my first head coaching job.

The chance to play professionally was at my feet, and I had to choose between the National Football League or the new World Football League, a tough choice. Every kid who has ever carried a football wants to play in the NFL, and I was no different. It had been my dream, but my situation now was different because I was selected so low in the draft by the Steelers. The decision about where to play wouldn't be simple.

My first thoughts were of my first year at Missouri wasted in that wishbone offense. That experience had cost me critical exposure of my true talents as a running back. The NFL scouts evaluated me only by what they saw, so when they didn't see me play as much as I could have, it put a question mark on my ability as a player. The Steelers' personnel director, Tim Rooney, said to me, "We knew that you would get drafted based on your accomplishments in junior college. We just didn't know what happened to you at Missouri." I thought a low draft selection meant that my talents weren't being respected. Although I had earned the honor of being drafted in the NFL, I was upset that teams did not see enough of my talents playing at Missouri to be considered a higher draft selection by the Steelers.

I was also troubled by the decision I had made not to protest the NFL rule about turning pro as I planned to when I came out of junior college. At the time, there had been people encouraging me to contest the rule for an early draft entry to the NFL, but during those years doing so was unheard of. Nevertheless, I wanted to pursue it. I sought the advice of a friend from back home named Bennie McRae, who played for the Chicago Bears. He put me in contact with his lawyers, who at first supported my case. Later, however, they backed out, and I dropped the issue.

When the question of Michael Vick leaving Virginia Tech to turn pro came up, I was very sensitive to his situation. It reminded me a lot of my own experience. It was difficult to advise him without bringing my own experiences into the decision, but I will discuss this more later in a chapter devoted to his story.

The decision about what league to play for went right down to the wire. I actually reported to a mini-camp with the Steelers along with the other draft choices in late May. I went to camp unsigned and had a very good workout with other newcomers like Lynn Swann, Lynn Stallworth, Mike Webster, and Donnie Shell. We stayed in the Marriott Hotel in downtown Pittsburgh. The sight of Three Rivers Stadium from the hotel window was breathtaking. I wanted to be a part of this organization more than anything.

An upcoming players' strike was stirring up controversy among all the players, but especially among the rookies. The top draft players like Swann, Stallworth, and Webster were assured of making the team, and would get no-cut contracts which would allow them to strike along with the rest of the team. Lower-round draft picks like myself were hung out to dry: We had to play hard, just hoping to make the team, and could be cut for any reason. I met veteran Steelers running back Frenchie Fuqua and quarterback Joe Gilliam while they were staying at the hotel. I was thrilled to meet them, but Fuqua would be a veteran player I would have to compete against for a spot on the team as running back.

I became friends with quarterback Joe Gilliam; he invited me to his room, and we talked about the strike. I told him about my situation, and that I was trying to decide whether to sign with the Steelers or play for the WFL. He said, "Look, Reamon, you 're a low-round pick. You can do everything right in camp, but when that strike ends and those veteran players report to camp, you'll get cut. I can't tell you what to do, but it will be tough for any rookie to make with this team this year."

His comments scared me a lot. After our talk, I felt strongly that even if I did sign with the Steelers, went to camp, and did well, and the strike ended, I would still have only a 50 percent chance to make the team. I did not want to gamble with my future, so I decided on a sure thing. I called Mr. Dwayne Jeter, the player personnel director for the Florida Blazers, and agreed on a contract. I reported to the World Football League's team camp held at James Madison University. They gave me a $4,000 bonus and a contract of $25,000. Little did I know that the WFL would turn out to be a play-for-*no*-pay experience. At the beginning of the season, a friend told me to defer my contract money for tax purposes, and I foolishly took his advice. I deferred my salary until December of that year, and had the rest of the salary paid in the month of January. The way things turned out, I went unpaid.

Life was repeating itself. When I came out of high school, the low SAT score kept me from being recruited by the big school and forced me to go to junior college, and now this—another detour to get to where I wanted to be in the NFL. The route from high school to the big school had so many twists and turns, and now the journey from college to the NFL seemed to be taking the same route. In both cases, I had to prove my worth and talents even with all I had already accomplished. I had to do it all over again.

The head coach of the Florida Blazers was the former Redskins linebacker, the great Jack Pardee. He was a legend in his time and had gotten his tutoring from Hall of Famer, Coach George Allen of the Washington Redskins. He played linebacker for Coach Allen, and they both had the same philosophy: to play veterans with experience.

Immediately when I arrived at camp, because I was the youngest player on the roster, I knew I had to work and show the coaches what I was all about. The team consisted of many veteran NFL players, who had dreams of playing football again. The players were a testament to the belief that football is a game, played by men who love and respect it as a game. They played for that love of it. Because the WFL was in competition with the established NFL, it was going to be financially tough on the owners. However, there seemed to be room enough in the country for two professional football leagues. Two weeks before the start of the regular season, the team which everybody thought was going to be based in Norfolk changed ownership, and the new owner moved the team to Orlando and renamed it the Florida Blazers. When we got there, we discovered the team didn't have much of a home.

The now-famous Tangerine Bowl was hardly a major league facility; the new bleachers were not even declared safe by city officials until the day of the opening game. However, I was thrilled to have a second chance to be able to prove to myself that I could play professional football. I stayed in a Holiday Inn next to the practice facility by the airport in Orlando. The city's support was enthusiastic. The players would go throughout the city promoting the team, even wearing our uniforms to Disney World to get more support.

When the season got started, I was waiting for my chance to play. I did not think I would play a lot at the beginning of the season. I remember my breakout game against the New York Stars. The game was played in the mud and heavy rain. Being the type of runner I was, a slash and low-body control runner, I made cuts in the mud, and their defense had problems stopping me. I don't know if they were that bad or not, but they gave me a ton of confidence. It sure built up my spirits, and I felt like I was back in junior college again.

After the New York game, Coach Pardee started calling me his Larry Brown. Larry was an all-pro running back with the Washington Redskins, a former teammate of Pardee's and one of my idols. I had many talks with Pardee, and I became one of his favorite players. He would single me out as the youngest guy on the team. He used me as an example of a star rookie and a contributor. Those compliments motivated me, and I started believing everything he said. He would discuss how he came back from cancer to play again and how you can overcome any adversity. Knowing this, I became even closer to him. However, he was an all-business type of coach. He stressed defense, his forte, and a conservative, ball-control style offense. We had a veteran NFL quarterback from the University of Virginia in Bob Davis, and rookie receiver in Greg Latta out of Morgan State University. There were veteran NFL players like Jim Strong, Larry Grantham, Mel Farr, and Ricky Harris. Coach Pardee was able to take these players and mold them into a team.

His coaching style utilized a blend of veterans and talented rookie players he felt could make big plays. There were times when we lost a couple of games, and we needed the veterans to turn it around. It was a long twenty-game season. At one time, around Labor Day, we played four games in a twenty-one-day period. We played one game on a Thursday and then played again on Monday. The WFL schedule put a lot of pressure on our bodies, and Coach Pardee knew there were times when we would make mistakes. But if you believed in yourself, he wouldn't let you get down. He embodied that George Allen philosophy without being a "rah-rah" coach like Allen; nevertheless, he got behind you and believed in you.

As the chaos of playing without paychecks started, it was a distraction for many of the guys, but I didn't care because I was running for a different reason, not for a paycheck. As midseason approached, we were winning games, but I was broke. However, I quickly learned to budget money. The hotel I lived in was within walking distance from a McDonald's. A local business arranged it so we could eat there free. I would eat breakfast, lunch, and dinner at McDonald's. I was broke, and the only money I had was what I had saved of the $4,000 signing bonus.

I had two teammates who I remember clearly had money problems: Greg Latta and a receiver named Hubie Bryant. Greg was a rookie like me and had a new white Cadillac and could not make the payments; it was repossessed. Hubie told me that he had picked up his paycheck from the team's office in the morning, and he had to pay his mortgage payment back home in Pittsburgh. Before the afternoon practice, the team's general manager came by the practice facilities and interrupted our team meeting to inform us that the payroll checks couldn't be cashed. He went on to say that one of the team's investors had been arrested on a drug conspiracy charge, and the team's president, Mr. Rommie Loudd, was implicated in the case. The banks had put a hold on their accounts until the case was investigated and cleared. Therefore, the checks that had just been issued were worthless.

Hubie yelled at the general manager, "Look man, I wrote checks out for my bills, and now you're telling me that the check you gave me is no good?"

In addition to the no-pay issue, there were rumors about the team moving to Atlanta or Tampa Bay. Here we were undefeated, the crowds were okay, and everything about Orlando seemed fine to me. The only time the owner would meet with the team was when the paychecks started to bounce; otherwise, we never saw him, and I never trusted him. The players would meet three times a week to keep the guys' spirits up and keep the season going. The veterans would intervene and talk the team up, and Coach Pardee would spend time in the office trying to hold it all together.

I remember one time, the owner Rommie Loudd got the team together and told us that Arab oil sheiks were coming to Florida to put a lot of money into the team. As crazy as it seemed, we believed it. The players thought to themselves, "Well, why not?" We were desperate to believe anything. We had no money except the $200 the league would send us every few weeks to keep us fed. There were a lot of times when we thought we had to just go out and finish the season.

Before the 1974 playoffs we were 14-6 and had to play the Philadelphia Bells, who were 9-11. We were wondering if we would get paid and if we should play at all. There was news around the league that players weren't being paid and there were questions about whether there would even be playoffs. Coach Pardee was also caught in the money issue, but he kept telling us to stay focused. I'll never forget when the World Bowl game was to be played in Birmingham, and Pardee's wife was trying to come to see the game.

The airline wouldn't approve their credit card, and she couldn't make the trip. I remember thinking, "Wow, it finally hit home. It even got to the coach."

The coach showed us how to stay focused by ignoring the disappointment. Coach Pardee said regularly in team meetings, "Each one of you must make up your mind to separate your problems off the field from your problems on the field." Sure, the players were worried about pay, but the adversity was bringing us closer together. So, despite the distractions, we made up our minds to win, no matter what happened. As a result, I broke my own rushing record with 189 yards rushing against Charlotte, with a 15-11 victory.

Fifteen weeks had now passed without paychecks. I was having a great season, and I didn't care if I ever got paid. I was reliving my junior college days, but now it was happening in the pros. I got such satisfaction from doing something I loved. I even had the chance to play against my brother, Charles. He played defensive back for the Birmingham Americans, and was faster than me. He was a great

Sister Willie, Brother Charles, Tommy, and a proud Mrs. Reamon.

player who never got the respect and attention he deserved. I have always said if he had gone to a larger college in those days, he would have gotten the right type of exposure. When he was in college at the University of Maryland at the Eastern Shore, I would visit him on my college break and watch him run in track meets; I was so proud to see him be successful.

The week before we played Birmingham, Coach Pardee and my offensive coach, Fred O'Conners, would tease me every day at practice. They would ask me if I talked to my brother, and joked, "Don't be giving your brother our game plan and tell him our secrets." The night we played against each other in Birmingham, our family traveled to the game with a busload of friends from our home. There were signs saying, "We support the Reamon boys" all over Legion Field Stadium. This night would be one of my greatest moments. He would hit me and I would say, "Good hit," and he would say, "Good run, bro."

On December 5, 1974, the WFL's only championship game, the World Bowl, took place. This was our biggest game, and it was on national television, with a crowd of 32,000 in the stands. We played the Birmingham Americans for the third time, but they had traded my brother to the Chicago Winds. That made me angry with their organization. They had gone unpaid for five weeks, and we hadn't been paid in thirteen weeks. On the game's first series of plays, we drove the ball down the field and I scored what seemed to be our first score. As I crossed the goal line, I was hit; and as I fell, the ball dropped to the ground and rolled out of the end zone. The television replay confirmed that I scored, but the officials ruled it a touchback. The Americans added to their lead, with the score now 22-0. Keeping pace with the craziness of the WFL's first season, the game was decided by a controversial touchdown.

If there was a time when we had to stay calm and play our game, this was it. I remember in the huddle, our quarterback Bob Davis was kneeling down on one knee, looking up at each of us. We showed frustration and concern, which resulted in our arguing among ourselves. He yelled, "Shut up! Shut up! We can still win this football game! We have to play our game. We can't go back."

In the third quarter, the never-say-die Blazers fought our way back on Bob's passing. He threw touchdown passes to Greg Latta and me to cut the lead to 22-14. WFL touchdowns were worth seven points, and we had failed to score both of our extra point attempts. The Birmingham team sent out their punting unit, and they punted to our punt returner, Rod Foster. The next few moments all 30,000 fans starred in disbelief as Foster returned the punt 76 yards for a touchdown. We now trailed 22-21. With time dwindling, they managed to run out the clock and win the WFL championship.

After the game I had to go back on the field to accept the World Football League's Co-Most Valuable Player Award. The other two players to receive the award were quarterback Tony Adams of Southern California Suns and fullback J. J. Jennings of the Memphis Southmen. We all appeared on camera in front of a national television audience with the commissioner Gary Davidson, who had an armored bank truck parked at the end of the field. Suddenly, an armed security guard approached at a short distance behind us with a bag of money. The commissioner made an announcement that the money in the bag would be given to us. The bag contained $10,000 in cash received from the game's gate receipts, to be split up three ways. The total equaled $3,333.33 for each of us. After the announcement, the commissioner told each of us that we had an option to take a check in the amount of the $3,333.33, or to take a free round-trip ticket for two to the Caribbean Islands. I was mentally and physically drained from the game, and hurting with a partially dislocated shoulder. I told the representatives that I accepted the money. As I headed home after the World Bowl, I knew that I wasn't going to continue as a Florida Blazer. I wanted to go with Jack Pardee. I knew he was headed to the NFL, and that's where I wanted to go too.

I returned to Newport News with a new set of goals to put in action. The first goal was to complete my college degree. I did not want to return to Missouri to finish school, so I transferred my college credits to Hampton Institute, now Hampton University. I needed two semesters' worth of college credits to graduate with a degree in Recreation and Leisure Studies. I enjoyed my off-season by attending school. I felt that the most important example for a student athlete to set was to have his or her college degree.

I spent my last semester in an internship at the World War II Recreation Center, where I had spent many after-school hours as a boy. The supervisor in charge of my internship at the center was my childhood friend Robert Dixon. It felt great to come back and work in the community, and I had the opportunity to put my second goal into action: to start a youth summer football camp.

The objective of the camp was to give youths an opportunity to meet pro players and learn the fundamentals of the game of football in an atmosphere of fun and fellowship. The focus was to help those kids who could not afford to attend a camp. The first thing I did was talk with local high school football coaches. The interest was great. I began to contact professional football players, and various businesses in the community for support, athletically and financially. The pro players who worked at the camp in the first year were former fifteen-year NFL veteran quarterback Norm Snead from Warwick High School, and Franco Harris of the Pittsburgh Steelers. I spent three months preparing for the camp's week of activities. I mailed out camp brochures to every high school in the state of Virginia. I spoke at selected elementary, middle, and high schools. I used a mailing list to contact all the Departments of Recreation and Little League and Pop Warner football organizations in the Tidewater area of Virginia. I had an agreement with the Department of Social Services to select youths from their programs throughout the area. The Social Services department matched one half of the cost of the camp with any other business that was willing to make a tax-deductible contribution for the youths in attendance. Robert Baskowitz, Mr. B from Missouri, donated $5000 dollars.

In addition, I spent my own money. The cost to organize and operate the camp yearly was between $5,000 and $8,000. It was very difficult in those days to find corporate sponsors the way we can today, so each year I contributed my own money to pay for many kids who could not afford to attend.

Financially the camp became a real problem for me because I had only managed to play one complete football season to earn all the money I would contribute in the camp's first three years of operation.

In June of 1975, after I had negotiated contract offers with the Pittsburgh Steelers, who owned my NFL rights, and the Toronto Argonauts of the Canadian Football League, I signed a one-year contract worth $100,000 with the Jacksonville Express of the World Football League. I was very happy to go back to the state of Florida. I received a $25,000 bonus—it was the largest amount of money that I had ever had. Immediately after signing the contract, I departed for Jacksonville, where preseason camp began that weekend. I asked my mother to deposit the check in the bank, and she called me in Florida to say, "Tommy I have never been so nervous to put money in the bank. I have never had a check that large in my hands."

I replied, "Mama, there will be many more of those deposits."

The contract that I signed was called a personal service agreement with the owner of the Jacksonville Express. Again I was afraid that the WFL would fold, so I wanted to make sure that I was paid. The agreement stated that if the league stopped playing at any time, I would be paid immediately by the owner.

After the first game we played, I was named the WFL player of the week for my performance against the Birmingham Vulcans, who had changed their name when a new management team took over. I gained 128 yards on 24 carries and scored 2 touchdowns. Then, five weeks into the season, I hurt my ribs in a game against the Philadelphia Bells.

I remember I could not breathe very well. I let the trainers talk me into taking a shot of cortisone in my back where the ribs were hurting, and I felt okay for a few minutes in pregame warm-ups. When the game started I began to run and could not catch my breath. The trainer suggested that I drink a can of Coca-Cola. I did and I could breathe a little better. However, I did not play the remainder of the game, and I went right home after the game. During the middle of the night my roommate awoke me to say that I sounded like I was having trouble breathing. I was concerned.

Trophies and souvenirs from a pro careeer, kept at
Tommy's mother's house in Newport News.

The next morning I went to the hospital emergency room. The doctor examined my ribs and listened to my breathing. He said my lungs had collapsed.

I asked how that could have happened, and he explained that the cortisone injection that the trainer had given me accidentally punctured a lung. He told me he had to fill my lungs back up. I really didn't comprehend what he had said. I just assumed that he would have me inhale through a tube or something, but when I asked the doctor how was he going to fill up my lungs, He said, "I will put a tube in your chest and fill them up that way." That made sense.

I checked into the hospital. I remember that I was singing and thinking good thoughts of just getting this thing over with, so I could go back to playing football. The doctor entered the room. The nurse cleaned off my chest area. I asked the doctor if he was going to sedate me. He said, "No, because you must be breathing normally for me to do this operation."

I will never forget the next couple of things that happened. The doctor made a small incision in my chest. He then began to push the tubes down into my chest, navigating with a tube in and around everything. I was screaming and yelling like I was dying. It was the worst pain I have ever experienced. The scar on my chest today keeps me reminded of that collapsed lung surgery in Jacksonville, Florida. If this kind of incident occurred today in sports, I would bet that the team doctor who accidentally punctured a lung while giving a cortisone injection would be sued

Today when I talk to my players about the world of football, I stress the importance of understanding how it has developed into big business. When players reach the college and professional levels, football is not just a game anymore. In my time, I failed to understand this. During my college and professional career I made several decisions based not upon what was best for my career but on personal feelings and relationships with players or coaches. The most successful players, however, approached their decisions like business decisions. I always thought with my heart, not with my head, and doing so led to several major disappointments.

My players must understand that if it is their goal to play college or professional ball, they will face very stiff competition for a few spots. With that in mind, I ask them first, "What is it you want from football?" If they want just the fun of high school football, then I try to see to it that they get it. For those who see it as a way to future success, I teach them from the beginning to approach it as if it were a business. The product they are selling is their skills, which they must fully develop in order to compete. I try to give them an idea of which skills and behaviors will be viewed as assets by the scouts, and which ones will be seen as liabilities. I teach them how to maximize their marketability. They must know that in the world of college and professional football, they will become a commodity.

Playing for the Chiefs, Tommy takes flight against the Bengals.

5. My Football Career Ends. Hollywood, Here I Come.

The WFL went bust in 1975. However, I had signed the personal service contract with Jacksonville's owner, which meant I got paid my salary. As soon as the WFL folded, the Steelers wanted to sign me. It sounded good, but if I signed with them, I had to forfeit my personal service contract, and their deal was no better than what I would have made from Jacksonville. While we were in negotiations, the Steelers went on to win their second straight Super Bowl.

So, in 1976, after the preseason, and though I had never played with them, the Pittsburgh Steelers traded me to the Kansas City Chiefs. I was not happy with being traded, but the Steelers just proved once again that football is a business. The year with the Chiefs would be my only complete season playing in the NFL, but I did not enjoy it. I also hurt my knee, which would require surgery. At the end of the season with the Chiefs, I found myself lying in a hospital bed in Kansas City, Missouri, recovering.

When my head coach with the Chiefs, Paul Wiggins, came by to see me, I did the unthinkable. Instead of the team trading me away without my say, I asked him to trade me to the Chicago Bears, so that I could play for my former WFL coach, Jack Pardee.

"Why, Tommy?" he asked.

I answered him, "Coach, I am too young not to be enjoying myself playing this game I love, and all I want to do is try to improve. When I was traded here by the Steelers I was so excited and thankful to you."

But even though I was grateful for the opportunity, I had never really wanted to return to Missouri to play football because of my experience there in college. The management did not like the fact that I refused to play with them in 1974, opting to play in the World Football League. In that year I was the WFL's leading rusher and MVP, but the Steelers won the Super Bowl. In 1975, I had to negotiate again with the Steelers because they had my college draft rights. The negotiations were full of egos and arrogance, centering around who needed whom. I asked the Steelers throughout our negotiations to trade my draft rights to Jack Pardee, and they refused. At one point, I thought a trade deal was imminent with the Bears, but I got a call from Coach Pardee and he said, "Tommy, the Steelers asked for too much in the negotiations. I'm sorry, we couldn't work out a trade deal for you."

I said to Coach Wiggins, "Do you want to know what the Steelers' general manager Dan Rooney said to me? He jabbed his fingers in front of my face and said, 'Tommy you were *that close* to getting back with your man,'" referring to Coach Pardee. I felt that Mr. Rooney made that comment in spite. I told Coach Wiggins about all the negotiations that had gone on behind closed doors with the Steelers.

After the 1976 Super Bowl Champions' season I agreed to a deal with the Steelers. Unfortunately, I was verbally chastised by various players about my refusal to play for them the previous two years. The receiver coach, Lionel Taylor, told me that the management did not like the fact that one of their college draft picks refused to play for them. In return, they would not do anything for me. So, from that comment by Mr. Rooney, I knew the Steelers weren't going to trade me to Coach Pardee and the Chicago Bears. Instead, the Steelers did what I least wanted. They sent me back to Missouri and the Kansas City Chiefs. That's how Rooney broke my heart. But like I said, I learned an important lesson. Football is a cruel business. At any rate, I did not want to play for the Chiefs.

Wiggins looked at me very strangely, and said, "I feel like I am selling a piece of property."

I replied to him, "Coach, I have never had a leg injury before, and the way I feel now, I don't want to play football next season."

"Tommy, I will see what I can do," he said compassionately.

In the end, the Chiefs traded me to the Bears. I was elated, but I also felt guilty that I had not given myself the chance to make things work out in Missouri. In retrospect, I made a bad decision. Nevertheless, I looked forward to a reunion with Coach Pardee. I knew that the decision to play with the Bears would be emotional because they had a great running back in Walter Payton. I didn't feel threatened by his talents, however. The benefit for me was the relationship I felt I had with Jack Pardee. Also, Assistant Coach Fred O'Conners would be a player's coach and friend to me.

I spent many weeks there in mini-camps conditioning my legs and weightlifting. Once Walter Payton took me out to dinner. He and I shared some stories about how we both ended up playing in the NFL and for what teams and coaches. Walter told me that he knew so much about me even before we met. He said, "When I first came to the Bears' training camp to watch films, the only football footage Coach Pardee had was of the Florida Blazers. I learned his offensive system by watching you."

In response, I told him the story of how the Steelers traded me away from Chicago and Coach Pardee. Coach Pardee said that they would draft a running back named Walter Payton instead. He laughed, and we just kept talking.

I told Walter about the summer football camp that I had started in Virginia, and asked him if he would attend. He agreed, and came to camp the next year. The kids loved him. He would do his workout for the day by running 25-yard sprints. Some of the kids started challenging him to races. After a few warm-up sprints, he had at least twenty kids lined up in two single lines to take him on two at a time.

He gave each line of kids a ten-yard lead, and in this way, he showed the kids his competitive spirit. Walter worked hard to catch and beat each one of them. He ran against all ten rows of kids and won. I remember an incident one evening at bedtime. The kids had a curfew, and had to be in their rooms. He and All-Pro defensive lineman "Mean Joe" Greene of the Super Bowl Champion Pittsburgh

Walter Payton (center) was among the famous guests at the Tommy Reamon Football Camp in its day.

Steelers went around the dormitory rooms opening doors to various rooms and rushing into the room to start pillow fights. One of the smaller kids started getting the best of them, so they took him into the bathroom and showered him down. The kids were so hyper for the rest of the night that nobody got much sleep.

The next morning at breakfast, everyone was still talking about the incident. The camper who got showered entered the cafeteria and got a round of applause from the other campers. I remember the camper jumping up on the cafeteria table and yelling out, "I beat up on Mean Joe and Walter Payton!" The foot races and pillow fights were highlights of the week's activities at the camp, and really showed Walter's spirit.

Just recently, I was shopping at a local store and a gentleman approached me and asked who I was. I identified myself.

He said, "I attended your football camp the year that Walter Payton was there. I still tell people today that Walter was so fast and how he outraced almost the whole camp while he was there."

To have this gentleman say those words to me about the camp, almost thirty years later, made me appreciate having that very small relationship with one of the greatest football players who ever played the game.

Coach Pardee and I had talked many times about playing together again. I was so excited to be back with him in what I thought would be the right environment. He was a player's coach and had the personality and character to bring a team together, and he had spent quality time with each individual player. In the WFL, with all the problems we were experiencing, he stressed that no one will believe in you more than yourself. He knew of the personal disappointments I had had in the past, and each day at practice he would say to me, "Give your best today, Tommy." During the financial problems in the WFL, he had talked with me about his battle with cancer. He often said, "My life was turned upside down and now, more then ever, I have to stay focused." Because he talked about his harrowing experiences, I made it a priority to put my past behind me and work for the future.

Pardee was honest with me when I arrived at the Bears' camp. He said, "Tommy, work hard, because I know you can play." I was learning their offense from a great quarterback coach named Sid Gilman. He was a legend in his own right and would continue to be the creator and developer of great offensive passing systems in the NFL for years to come. I spent hours working with him, listening and preparing for the start of summer practice.

When camp started, I was in great shape, and I knew I had to work hard to make the team, despite my relationship with Coach Pardee. The camp was held in Lake Forest, Illinois, a suburban area north of Chicago. The weather was cool, which enticed me to practice harder. My legs burned with exertion, and I was worn out after every practice. I lifted before practices to strengthen my injured knee, but my legs felt heavy. I was concerned about my quickness.

One day after practice Coach O'Conners asked me, "Tommy, are you okay? You move like you've lost a step in your lateral movement when hitting the line of scrimmage."

"Yes, Coach, I'm okay, but I do feel tired a lot," I responded. I knew I was going to have trouble making the team after that conversation. I was having a pretty good preseason camp, but the depth chart posted each day told a different story. I was on the third unit at running back, but I was participating on the punt returns and kickoff return teams. However, a veteran running back named Mike Adamle, who had been injured in the off-season, was expected back during the season. I lived with a feeling of urgency to do well to make the team. The last preseason game I played in was against the New Orleans Saints. On the first kickoff return of the game I scored right up the middle for 85 yards.

I was excited, but still worried. I expected the team roster cuts to be posted in the next few days, and I could only hope for the best. Two days later, General Manager Jim Finks called me in. In a very businesslike way, he said, "Tommy, we will have to let you go."

With that statement, my dreams crumbled. The decision was made because the team was planning to keep a running back spot on the team for Adamle. I told him I did not know what was next for me. I did not even want to talk to Coach Pardee. Mr. Finks suggested that the head coach with the Saskatchewan Roughriders of the Canadian Football League had called, and would like me to come there to play. I thanked him and left a phone number where I could be reached if anyone wanted to contact me. I had cousins in Chicago who came to see me play, and when I was released from the Bears, I stayed in their home until I got a call to go try out in Saskatchewan. I left my car with my cousins Marjorie and Irwin; my brother Charles would fly to Chicago and drive it back to Newport News. I was headed to Canada. I did not have time to feel sorry for myself.

I began to play for the Roughriders within a week, and lived in a hotel for nearly a month. The first game I played in, I scored on the first play of scrimmage for 50 yards and immediately made a name and impact on that team. It was just like the WFL, but the players were not as talented. The playing rules were a little different, and they pressured the United States players to perform well. I reinjured my knee and was sidelined for at least two games, but the four or five games I played in that green-and-white uniform were spectacular. However, after weeks of nursing an injured knee, I began to lose enthusiasm. Suddenly, the team released me; I really did not know why, because I was doing so well for them.

I was ready to leave Canada, but to go where? I had always dreamed of going to California. I had been there once, when the University of Southern California and UCLA were trying to recruit me. Since I had some friends there, this would be the best time to visit them and see some of the sites and stars of the sports and entertainment industries. I called a friend from Orlando, Trudy Stone, whom I had known from my days with the Florida Blazers. She and her family had moved to L.A., and I asked them if I could stay with them for a few weeks She said yes, and I got on a plane to Los Angeles. On the flight, I tried to plan out my future.

I wrote a letter to Coach Pardee thanking him for the opportunity to play for him again in Chicago. I said that I believed I could still play the game, and I asked him to talk to Coach George Allen, the head coach for the Washington Redskins, for me to see if they would give me an opportunity to try out for their team next season. I thought it was a long shot to get a tryout with the Redskins, but it was worth it to see if Coach Pardee could help me once again. I felt that if I could get one more chance to play the game that I loved, then why not let it be for a team that was close to my home in Virginia.

I spent my first days in Los Angeles sightseeing. I had always dreamed of working in the film industry as an actor, and I thought I would be especially good in sports-related shows. Having been a successful football player would help me to get the opportunity. My second week there, I went to Universal Studios and visited the stage sets where they shot many of the television shows and motion pictures. I went to the studio set that was filming the TV show *Kojak*. The first person I saw on the set was Telly Savalas. I walked up to him and introduced myself. We had met before at the Whitney Young Urban League banquet in New York City, introduced by a former professional football player named Buddy Young.

Mr. Savalas said, "Nice seeing you again. Buddy was a great friend of mine and if you need anything let me know." I told him I wanted to be an actor. He responded by saying, "Then hang around and meet some of my people, and we'll see what we can do." I thanked him. For him to even suggest helping me made the whole trip worthwhile.

I spent nearly three months at various studio sets learning how actors, producers, and directors perform their jobs. I studied and observed the workings of the television and film production industry with all the ambition of an aspiring young star. I took acting classes at the famous Lee Strasburg Institute of Acting. I felt as excited in this new career as I had felt playing football. I met a theatrical agent named David Wilder, a former college football player who was very popular among casting directors and producers of many TV shows and film production companies. David told me that I had to learn how to get around town and become acquainted with the people who could influence the future of a young actor. I did just that.

The first thing I did was hire the Dave Mirisch public relations firm. His company set up meetings, interviews, and entertainment events such as celebrity basketball and softball games and racquetball and tennis matches. I began going to the studios' private screenings and premieres of the upcoming shows and films. I enjoyed this life, and I was very good at presenting myself to the casting directors, producers, and directors who were important to the development and guidance of an actor. I always had a smile on my face and tried to let these people see that I could speak well.

I would later tell Aaron Brooks and Michael Vick that it was critical to let people see that great smile. I told them to visualize being in front of a camera, and encouraged them to practice those behaviors in front of the bathroom mirror at home. I constantly urged upon them to rehearse interviews so they would know how to act in those situations.

I remember my first acting job. The producer of *Kojak*, Matthew Rapt, saw me on the studio set one day and said, "Tommy we've *got* to use you in one of our shows before the television season is over."

"Yes sir!" I responded, surprised and delighted.

"Come see me tomorrow at my office and let me try to use you in our next episode."

I was so excited that I called my agent and told him to contact the *Kojak* show casting director. The next evening, I had two messages on my answering machine. The first call was from David Wilder, my acting agent. He said, "Tommy, you got an acting job with the *Kojak* show." I really appreciated what Mr. Rapt had done; he was a man of his word.

The second message stated that I was to call the new head football coach of the Washington Redskins, named *Jack Pardee*. I yelled so loud with the words, "Thank you, Lord!" I was shocked by this news. I'd had no idea that he was a candidate for the coaching position. I immediately telephoned Coach Pardee. We talked for a few minutes about working together again and I remember saying to him, "Coach, I will make you proud." He responded, "I know you will, Tommy." I was so excited to have a chance to play again the next season. However, I was also glad to have found a new career that I liked as much as football.

I spent four months hustling after acting jobs. I landed about six shows; they were small character roles, but I never did land enough big roles to help me pay my bills. I decided to find an evening job, since I wanted to keep my days free for my acting career. I started to work for a top security company, owned and operated by a man named Pete Stafford, a former Los Angeles police officer. He would become my closest friend and mentor. His company worked at the big Hollywood events such as the Oscars and Grammy Awards. Mr. Stafford was very respected in the police community, and with this connection, he provided private security and investigations for celebrity entertainers. I learned a lot about the security business world from my relationship with him, but I did not want to make it a career. I worked as a security officer backstage during the Academy Awards show for three years. I had a chance to meet and have nice conversations with many of the industry's top performers, including Diana Ross, Dolly Parton, and Michael Jackson.

Rough Diamonds

After six months in Hollywood, I returned home to Newport News to prepare for the summer football camp and preseason practice with the Washington Redskins. My own camp was in its fourth and, it turned out, final year of operation. I decided I could no longer afford the financial commitment and preparation time to continue operating it, especially since I would be going back to L.A. after the football season was over. I was very proud of myself at that year's camp because I would be playing with the Redskins. I advertised the camp in the local newspapers and received a greater response from more kids than in any other year. The other pro football players that year were Dan Pfeiffer of the Chicago Bears, Dallas Hickman of the Washington Redskins, and Hall-of-Famer Willie Lanier of the Kansas City Chiefs. I had a great staff of high school coaches who worked at the camp each year—Freddie Mitchell, who handled the local chapter of the Fellowship of Christian Athletes program, with Bob Schmidt, Ted Bacote and my brother, Charles, a former pro defensive back.

After the week-long camp activities ended, I was headed to Washington. I was nervous my first day of practice. Many of the veteran players would tease me about my acting career in Hollywood. Joe Theismann and I talked about the movie business and the lifestyles these people lived. Joe wanted to get into the acting business also. He was well known as a successful pro player, and had the charm and the charisma to handle the Hollywood life.

I watch him now, twenty years later, as an ESPN football commentator, and his personality really comes across on camera. He is having fun, but he has not changed one bit in the opinion department. Theismann was a great athlete, but in this 1978 season, he was competing against the old man Billy Kilmer for the starting QB position. Theismann had the youthful new general manager Bobby Beathard in his corner, and Kilmer, the old pro with that famous flying duck throwing pass, had coach Pardee on his side. Pardee preferred to play veteran players. I had experienced that with him in the old World Football League. And now Pardee and Beathard fought with each other over who would be the starting QB. Theismann and Beathard won out, and a new era began for Joe Theismann. The battle for player personnel control for the Redskins had just begun to heat up between Beathard and Pardee.

I knew that if I was going to make the team, I had to perform better than a few young draft picks that the new general manager favored. Beathard came to the job from the Miami Dolphins, where his position as player personnel director had earned him a lot of publicity. He claimed to be the personnel guru who helped develop the great Miami teams that included the 1972 season that saw them go undefeated all the way through the Super Bowl. He had the reputation of being a great evaluator of a player's talent. I remember reading an article around the time he accepted his job that quoted him as saying, "I will select the best available player in this year's NFL draft. They will also be able to play on the special teams." He did just that; he drafted a running back, punt and kickoff returner named Tony Green out of the University of Florida.

The second week of summer practice I broke my right thumb. I was pass blocking on a linebacker and my thumb got caught underneath his shoulder pads. I couldn't believe my bad luck. The other running backs in camp were Mike Thomas, John Riggins, and Clarence Harmon. These players were all going to make the team. Even though I had a cast on my right hand, I could still catch the football, but I had to carry the ball in my left hand. I could not help but think about my broken left hand at Missouri. Nevertheless, I was in great running shape.

One day after practice Coach Pardee said to me, "Tommy you are looking real good. Keep it up." I was thrilled to hear this comment from him. I was practicing almost all the time, and even with a cast on my hand, I was still putting in more time than the other backs. But it seemed that Clarence Harmon and I were the only healthy backs in practice daily. John Riggins and Mike Thomas were the starters, but they were plagued by injuries. The rookie Tony Green pulled a hamstring and did not practice for days. There were days when I walked off the practice field physically exhausted. I had promised myself, if this was going to be my last chance at playing professional football, I was going to give every ounce of energy in my body.

Today I tell my senior players that they will never relive the playing experience of their high school years. Therefore, they must give it their all. Each day they should practice as though it were their last. For instance, I often tell them about Hosie's sudden death, then ask them if they think he would have played even harder if he had known it would be his last time on the field.

The third preseason game was against the Green Bay Packers. I started at running back and Joe Theismann was the quarterback. Even with the cast on my right hand, I put on my best performance in my short career in the NFL. In the fourth quarter, Theismann and I put on a show. In the winning drive I carried the ball three straight times, gaining 35 yards. Theismann hit me with a flare pass out of the back-field, and I caught it and turned the left corner of the end zone and scored. I was so happy over my performance.

After the game, I went looking for Coach Pardee. I looked at him with a big smile on my face. He returned the smile and said, "I hope this performance is enough." I was so happy that I totally missed what his comment truly meant. In the Newport News *Daily Press* in August 1978, an article written by Bob Moskowitz appeared, which read:

Reamon, Skins Ready for Colts

The Washington Redskins' defense is tough. I mean really tough. We have a great secondary. I didn't notice exactly what position the lineman were in, I just noticed they were there!" Making the somewhat prejudiced claims is Tommy Reamon, the classy little running back from Newport News who raised a lot of eyebrows in last week's 20-12 preseason Washington conquest of Green Bay. Reamon was an unexpected starter for ailing Mike Thomas. The Redskin running back goes into tonight's visit to Baltimore's Memorial Stadium still contending with a stomach virus. Reamon was saying the other night he had no idea whether or not he'll get another shot as a starter. "It depends entirely how Thomas feels," he said. Reamon, who won't shed a cast on a broken right thumb until Monday, carried 20 times for 75 yards and a touchdown.

I did not play against the Colts. The rookie running back Tony Green played. That Monday I was called into Coach Pardee's office. Despite all my hard prayer that this moment would never come, I saw what was happening when he shut the door. As soon as I took my fifth step into the office, he said, "Tommy, I thought you had it this time. I sure was pulling for you." Tears came flowing down my face. I took a deep breath and said, "Coach, I have spent my entire career trying to play for you. If you really cared for me, you could have said, 'Tommy, stay where you are.' You could have told me to stay in L.A. At Chicago, you could have told me to stay in Kansas City. But you didn't, and I trusted you with my life. That trust may be my fault, but you could have helped me more along the way, by just saying, 'Tommy, no.'"

He responded, "Tommy, this is so difficult for me too. I just could not control the outcome."

This scene would play out in my mind for the next twenty-five years. In the year 2002, a story was written in the Roanoke *Times* about Michael Vick and my relationship with him titled "Man and Mentor." In the article, the reporter Mike Hudson interviewed Jack Pardee. Pardee, now retired in Texas, said that at the time, he didn't want to me to go, but he didn't have the authority to make the call. "If I'd been doing the whole thing myself," Pardee said, "there wouldn't have been any doubt about it."

That meeting with Coach Pardee comes to mind whenever I watch the movie *North Dallas Forty*, in which I play the role of goody two-shoes Delma Huddle. At the end of the movie, the main character, played by actor Nick Nolte, meets with the head coach and is informed that he is no longer on the team. While the movie conveys the message of "win at any cost," I saw the theme of football as a business run by businessmen, with the athletes as products that give the public entertainment for a profit.

Because of money, power, and competition in professional sports, a team's management relationship with its players is about business. Today I see this demonstrated by a team's ability to win games and pay the money to the players who can help it accomplish that. I used to feel that football was a game, but I have since realized how brutal the business side is. As I look back now on my emotional attachment to Coach Pardee, I realize he had a job to do, and he could do only so much for me on a personal level. He did not have the power to make the decisions on all personnel matters. Today in the NFL, the head coach wants complete control of football player personnel matters, but not many are able to get it.

After I was released from the Redskins, I went home to Newport News, my football career over. I decided to drive my car to Los Angeles to get back to acting. I was very thankful that I had a direction in life, and I thought a long trip across the country would do me good. I visited Las Vegas on the way, and called home to talk to my mother. When she answered the phone, she said, "I am glad you called, because your agent in Los Angeles called and said for you to call him immediately."

I responded, "I hope he can find some work."

After I talked a while with Mama, I called David Wilder. He answered the telephone, "How you doing, Tommy?"

I said, "I'm doing better than I was a few days ago."

"I just wanted to call and see how you were doing. Look, you keep your head up and when you get in town, come see me when you are ready to work," he said, saddened but positive, like an undertaker giving comfort to a distraught family member.

I finally got my big character role in the football movie by Paramount Pictures named *North Dallas Forty*. The way I earned the role of Delma Huddle is more interesting than actually performing it on the big screen was. One day I was walking onto the lot of Paramount Pictures Studios and the gate attendant, who had heard that I was a former pro football player, stopped me and said, "Have you heard about a football movie we are planning to make?"

I got excited and said, "No, but do you know who the producers are?"

"I heard Frank Yablans, do you know him?"

"Not yet!"

I immediately went looking for the producer's offices on the studio lot. I called my agent David Wilder and the Dave Mirisch public relations firm. I told them to find out who the producers of this football movie were. I didn't have to wait long before Dave Mirisch called me and said, "The casting director of that football film is in my office building on the second floor! You can come by my office and I will take you to meet him."

I did not waste any time; I wanted to meet the people involved in this football film the next day. I stopped by the casting director's office in hopes of introducing myself. As I entered the office, I was met by the secretary at the reception desk. I said, "Hello, my name is Tommy Reamon, and Dave Mirisch from upstairs in your building," I pointed up, "suggested to me to stop by your office to introduce myself to the casting director of the football movie that Paramount Pictures is planning to shoot."

"The casting director's name is Reuben Cannon," she said, then, "You have to have your agent contact him, to set up a meeting." I responded quickly, "Well, I think they have spoken, that's why I am here, but can you check with him, please, and tell him that I'm the former professional football player turned actor, interested in the football movie?" The secretary asked me to have a seat, and went to see.

While I was waiting, I started looking for something to read. Suddenly my eyes focused on the reception desk. A screenplay was lying there, with the title *North Dallas Forty.* Dave had told me the title when we talked on the phone, so I immediately grabbed it and started reading. My heart was beating fast as I thumbed through it. I made a bold decision: I took the screenplay out of the office into the hallway to read it more. As I stood there reading the script, I was interrupted by some people getting off the elevator. They walked toward me, then entered the casting director's office.

I did not want to go back into the office with the script because the secretary might see that I took it, so I decided to take it up to Dave Mirisch's office. As I walked up to his office door I noticed a sign on it saying, "Out to lunch and will return in one hour." Well, now I had a choice to make: return the screenplay to the casting director's office, or keep it. I decided to keep it and take it home to read.

The next day I called David Wilder to find out if he had contacted the casting director for the project. I felt too embarrassed to tell him that I had gone by their office and taken a copy of the screenplay. When David answered the phone, he said "Tommy, I have great news, I was going to call you today. I have set up an interview with the producer and director of the film to see you for the character role of Delma Huddle. They will see you next week." I was glad now that I had decided to keep the screenplay. I felt guilty, but I wanted that part.

The day of my interview, I was so pumped up that it felt like I was preparing for a football game. I was nervous and I had the same tightness in my stomach; I liked this challenge. I was interviewed by the producer, director, and casting director. Each one of them took a turn asking me to read a couple of lines from the script. I was ready and prepared with all my lines. At the end of the interview, they asked me some questions about my days as a football player. The director, Ted Kotcheff, was excited over my reading. "You did well," he said, "I liked your performance." They told me that they would be in contact with my agent and they looked forward to working with me. I didn't know how to take their comments about working with me, but I walked out of that office and jumped up in the air as though I had just scored a touchdown.

I still felt guilty about taking the screenplay, and eventually told my agent about it. He said, "No big deal, but you shortened the audition process a little."

I worked on the set of *North Dallas Forty* for three months. The film was released with premiere screenings in Los Angeles and in Newport News. I enjoyed the exposure, and felt appreciative and thankful to the many people who had continued to follow me as I changed careers from football to acting. My longtime friend Mr. Melvin Price, the Budweiser distributorship owner, paid for a hundred people to attend my welcome-home screening of the movie. He had honored me in the same way in my senior year of football at Missouri, when he had paid for sixty of my family and friends to take a bus trip to the University of North Carolina at Chapel Hill to see me play.

The success of the movie did have an effect on my acting career. I continued to get small roles in television shows while I worked in security to pay my bills, but this was the first year I did not have the financial resources to keep my summer football camp open for the kids back home. I had discontinued the camp with great regret, but now I had the idea that I wanted to tell the story of my kids' camp experience. For years I had told friends in the industry about how I returned to Virginia each summer to operate the camp.

After the success of the *Bad News Bears*, a movie about a group of kids coming together from different backgrounds to play baseball, I was inspired to tell the story of my camp. It was perfect: The camp featured professional football players as instructors, and the kids who attended came from all over the country and from lots of different backgrounds, all with their own reasons to attend, but with the common goal of meeting professional players.

Sylvester Stallone's story also influenced me. He'd had to fight every step of the way to make *Rocky* by himself, but it was a huge hit. This inspired me enough to spend two years trying to get my movie made. I set out to learn all the details I needed to know to make a major motion picture. I used my own money and raised funds from family and friends to invest in the writing of the screenplay.

I was determined to make it work, or the industry would run me out of town trying. The working title was *Winners*. The writer was a first-time screenplay writer who did a good job on the early draft of the script. However, I found out fast that the industry does not like new and unproven writers.

I pursued professional actors to play various key character roles in the story in order to get the interest from a studio. I then talked to proven directors in the industry with histories of directing films with similar story lines. I located and visited with each potential director and actor I was interested in. The response time from these people and their agents was very frustrating. I personally visited or communicated with every major studio in Hollywood and around the country. I contacted top independent production companies and their project development divisions. The four issues that continued to surface throughout the selling of the project were the screenplay, the actors, the director, and distribution.

Once I had sent the screenplay to be reviewed, and it was declined, I could not go back to that studio without a rewrite of the script by a new writer. This was not easy because I needed money to hire a second writer. Then I had to find marketable actors for the major roles. The top young actors at that time were Matt Dillon, Scott Baio, and Doug McKeon, but to get any of these actors, a side deal with the agent had to be made. After I contacted and sent the screenplay to their agents, the agents' response would be, "My client is interested in the project; however, we want to know who is distributing the project." It was a catch-22 between the actor's agent, who wanted to know the studio, and the studio, who wanted to know the actors. If I could deliver one of them, the other would make a deal. NFL football players like Joe Montana were looked upon as non-actors, in the film industry's words, "not of marketable name value for major roles."

Landing an experienced director was equally frustrating. A director was as good as his or her last film job. The studio executives would say they liked this guy versus another guy, and I tried to contact whomever they suggested in order to find the right fit. My head was spinning with the effort just to get someone to say, "Yes, we will do your project."

Because I was draining my bank account, I decided to contact my old friend and University of Missouri football booster Robert

Baskowitz. The last words he had spoken to me after the Sun Bowl Game were, "If you ever need anything, let me know." Well, some five years later I decided to ask him for help.

I telephoned Mr. B. and reminded him immediately of that offer. "Mr. B., I am trying to produce a movie based on the kids' summer football camp I used to run, the one for the underprivileged that you once donated money to. It's a great story, sir."

"Tommy, how much money are we talking about?"

"The proposed budget to do the film project is 1.5 million dollars."

He paused a moment, then replied, "Well, Tommy, for that kind of money you need to come down to St. Louis and talk to me."

I traveled to St. Louis with Bob Joseph, a friend and business partner who was working with me on the project. I felt that it was important to bring someone with me who represented the business aspect of the film industry. Mr. B. was very respectful to me and direct about his concerns. "Tommy, I'm very proud of you for taking on this kind of challenge, but I want to be honest with you. I need to know how will I get my money back—furthermore, can you guarantee me that I ever *will* get it back?"

I replied, "I can't guarantee anything, but I believe our chances are great. With a distribution deal from a major studio company, we can't fail." I explained that the interest was there for this kind of general audience movie. If he agreed to give me a letter of intent to finance the movie, I could get a distribution deal. We needed to show the distributor that we had the money to do it; then they only had to distribute the film, and they would not have to finance the project. I knew we could get a distribution company. "This way, you will get your investment guaranteed, and the movie will get distributed." Mr. B. thanked me and asked for a few days to think about it.

I left St. Louis feeling good, and within two weeks I received a letter of intent for the amount of $1.5 million to finance my movie, subject to a distribution deal. I immediately went back to all the film studios that had turned me down earlier because of the screenplay, and questions on the story content, a marketable actor or director, and so on. This time I had the finances, subject to a deal from them. Orion Pictures and Paramount Pictures showed great interest. They began serious talks on a possible distribution. However, they still wanted a rewrite of the screenplay. I was disappointed to hear that again, but determined to solve the problem. As a strategy to help get the approval of the distribution deal for the film, I requested and selected a writer whose work was known by each of the studios.

I called Mr. B. and explained that the studios had requested a rewrite of the screenplay before they would agree to a distribution deal. I asked him if he would give me the funds for a new writer. He said no. I was surprised and felt a little uneasy with his abrupt answer, but I was determined to find a way to raise the funds to pay for the rewrite. I borrowed $60,000 dollars from friends and family and hired the new writer. The talks with each studio were intense as we all awaited the completion of the rewritten script. I was certain that the pieces were coming together to make the movie.

I was so confident that I began putting plans for the film's production into action. I rented an impressive office near Universal Studios in the name of T.R. Productions, Inc. With more meetings scheduled with the studio executives at Orion Pictures, they gave me the impression that the distribution deal would be forthcoming at the completion of the rewritten screenplay. Every day I anxiously anticipated the awaited script. After four weeks and a day passed, the script was finished and sent to the studio. Within a week, I got a call from both studios that the screenplay was good enough to go forward. I was elated, to say the least. I called Mr. B. in St. Louis, but he was out of the country on business. He was not due back for another week. I decided to call him anyway, and I contacted him at a hotel in Brazil. I told him the good news. He said, "Great news! I will be back home next week and you can come see me then." I was too anxious to wait in L.A., so I flew to St. Louis and stayed three days at a hotel he owned, waiting on his return.

When Mr. B. arrived at the hotel, we talked about the process of funding the production company. He told me that his attorneys needed to be in contact with the distribution company at this point. I said to him, "That's fine, Mr. B. Do you have a time when I can talk with your attorneys about the financial structure of funding the film?" He said, "No, but as soon as possible." I started feeling uncomfortable with the tone of his responses to my questions. I told him I would be happy to stay in St. Louis to help finalize the deal or answer any questions his attorneys might have. I stayed at his hotel in Clayton, Missouri, a suburban community near St. Louis, for a week. I felt that all my dreams were now resting in someone else's hands, and this made me even more uneasy. Was Mr. B.'s sudden evasive behavior setting me up for a letdown? I nervously awaited the outcome of his attorneys' investigation into the film project and their negotiations with the distributors. I called his attorneys several times to get an update. However, I got no information from them, and Mr. B. had gone out of town again.

I sat alone in his hotel, waiting. I debated whether to go back to L.A. to wait it out there, but I couldn't make myself go. Somehow I felt that by staying, I could make this dream come true. I wasn't ready to give up. I finally received a call from Mr. B.'s attorney informing me that the financial structure of Mr. B.'s hotel business would not allow him to make the commitment to an investment of this magnitude. He went on to say that they informed Mr. B. of their decision and he agreed with them. He stated that "He will call you in L.A. as soon he has returned to St. Louis." The hurt that I felt during and after that telephone call can't be expressed in words. I left St. Louis without seeing Mr. B., and he never did call me to explain why he did not fund my movie project.

I headed back to L.A. with tears in my eyes and a heavy heart. I was devastated and physically sick. This hurt was worse than what I had experienced when my coach and mentor Jack Pardee released me from the Washington Redskins. I found myself unable to find a way to handle it. Before, I had always been able to move forward; when one door closed, I had simply found another one to open and walk through. This time, all of my dreams had fallen apart, and for the first time in my life, I couldn't seem to find another door to open.

As a running back, when I got hit and lost yardage, the idea was to get the ball and try again. I would keep going until I broke into a long run and scored. But this time I was down, and I couldn't find a way to get up. I had no idea of how to start over. First my football career, and now my dreams of Hollywood were just so much dust scattered around me.

I experienced total depression, and I did not know how to handle such failure. My mother, worried about me, called every hour of the day to talk. I couldn't eat or sleep. I wanted an answer to why Mr. B. had backed out of the deal; it consumed me. One night I started having pain in my chest. At first, I tried to ignore the pain, but as the night went on, it became more severe. I was alone in my apartment. I didn't want to see anyone, and in fact, had refused calls from my friends for weeks. The pain became so severe, I thought I was having a heart attack. The strange thing was, I almost didn't care. I started coughing up blood, but before I could reach the telephone to get help, I blacked out. The next morning I woke up in the hospital with tubes in my arm. The doctor diagnosed me as being severely dehydrated from not eating, and I was bleeding from a hiatal hernia in my chest. I never understood the diagnosis, but I did know that I felt mentally unstable.

After my release from the hospital, my mother begged me to come home. However, I knew I had to dismantle all parts of the movie project. In my new office, I sat on the floor and stared at the walls for hours. I had no one to blame but myself for the naïve behavior I had demonstrated at times and the many mistakes I had made in the pursuit of making my story into a movie.

I spent the next three weeks trying to get my mind stable enough to close out any business deals that I had created with the film project. I decided to go back home to Newport News. I will never forget how hard it was to leave L.A. after such disappointment and failure.

In 1984 I left California and have never been back. On my return to Virginia, I stopped in Washington, D.C., to visit an old high-school girlfriend named Brenda Knight. I was still not ready to face my family, many of whom had helped me financially on my movie project.

How could I face these people who had believed in me enough to invest their hard-earned money in my dream? Brenda and I had stayed in touch throughout my football career, and she had come out to L.A. to visit me during my time living there. I desperately needed something to believe in. I had never been one to invest my dreams in a person, but now the time seemed right. Brenda was a good, caring person, and a personal relationship with her would be just the medicine for my broken heart. I was very vulnerable and undecided on what I wanted in my life at that time.

Brenda was a single parent raising her fourteen-year-old son, Dwayne. She gave me a direction to a new life that neither of us was aware of at that time. That direction would be the guidance and development of my first diamond in the rough. I had first met Dwayne when he was ten years old; Brenda had sent him to my kids' summer football camp. At that time I played with the Washington Redskins. Now I was a man about to become part of his personal life. Dwayne was in the ninth grade and already had a long rap sheet of school suspensions. He was not a good student, mainly due to behavior and discipline problems.

Brenda asked me to help give Dwayne some direction in his life, saying I would be a good male role model for him. However, I didn't know my own life's direction, so how in the world could I guide and help a troubled teenager? I had spent many years mentoring boys through athletics, but this situation was different. I was in the same house with Dwayne, and he really didn't show a lot of interest in sports.

I began to talk with him about sports and attitude. However, he saw me as a threat. Because I was having a relationship with his mother, he felt that I was trying to take away his special time with her. One evening he came in the house and didn't follow the directions that his mother had given him, and I spoke to him in a firm tone. He said to me, "You're not my daddy."

That statement hit me hard, and I reflected back on my on experiences with my stepfather. I could see him as a troubled kid trying to understand why his mother and I were trying to team up on him with discipline. I started to spend time with him and try to influence him to my way of thinking. I asked him if he wanted to be a star, and he said he did. I told him that if he did what I asked of him, I could make him a star. However, I told him he would have to move to Newport because I would be leaving to return home. During the weeks and months I had spent with Dwayne and Brenda, becoming more and more involved with Dwayne's life, I had begun to realize how much I enjoyed being there to guide him. It had started me thinking about a career change; there were so many kids like him who needed guidance, and I had always enjoyed working with them. My first objective was to obtain a teaching certificate, and to do so meant a return to school. I explained this to Dwayne.

Brenda had mixed emotions and some reservations, and wasn't ready to move right away, but supported me in my final decision. Leaving Brenda and Dwayne behind was difficult because they had become very important to me during a time of great stress in my life; however, I left feeling renewed and with a sense of purpose, something I hadn't felt in months. With that goal in mind I returned home to Newport News, enrolled at Hampton University, and never looked back. I had left California in mental anguish and with no sense of where I was going or what I would do. Now, three months later, I was able to put that life behind me and begin again.

Today I use that time in my life as an example to teach my players to see life's failures as stepping-stones to a better future. As an old running back, I tend to talk about life in football terms: I tell them that every time they touch the ball, they are going for a first down—that sometimes they will get pushed back, and other times they will get hit, but each time they must get up and go again for that first down. I tell them that if they can't break through the middle, go around the end. If they occasionally fumble the ball, they will get another chance to hold it tighter. Each time they touch the ball will bring new opportunities.

My failure in Hollywood had been just such an example. I learned from that experience to see it not as a failure, but merely as a chance to carry the ball in a different play—as a teacher and a coach. I use my own disappointments to show them how to keep going, keep their feet moving, and always push forward. Each failure has a purpose, a lesson it was sent to teach us, and we should see it as an opportunity to grow. Now I can look back at what I saw as the worst time in my life and see it as stepping-stones, leading me to where I was truly meant to be.

When Coach Reamon left Hollywood, he had to make a career move. He earned his teaching certificate and started coaching, and thank goodness he did. In this recent photo, Michael Vick leans in to talk strategy.

6. The Return Home, Beginning My Coaching Years

With my return to Newport News, I left behind everything that had been my life and I started over. My career would change from promoting myself to teaching and coaching student athletes. The path to becoming a teacher and coach would not be an easy one. I had to go back to school, take education classes, and then pass the national teacher examination to get certified. I began to talk with and visit various friends and local school administrators to get their input on the correct route to take in order to become a teacher.

But I had to stay guarded. I was very hesitant to inform anyone that I had failed in my movie career. I had a lot of pride, and was very sensitive about what people thought of me. Most people in Newport News were familiar with my acting success, and I wanted to remain a success in their eyes. I did not want them to look at me as a failure, to categorize me as another former sports player who lost all his money, if and when they were told the true reason I returned home.

I started working for a security company at night so I could go to school during the day. I was ashamed of the security job because I felt that people would assume that I was not doing well and that I did not have a college degree. Nevertheless, I was determined to get a teacher's certificate and become a teacher and coach.

I spent a year working as a security officer at night and taking classes at Hampton University's graduate school. The school offered a program in which a college graduate like myself could get teacher certification in the field of Special Education with Learning Disabilities. I enjoyed taking these classes because they taught me how some students must have special help to allow them to be successful.

This field truly represented my belief that some students need individualized instruction, and that with the proper development and guidance, they can succeed. At the completion of the course requirements I had to pass the National Teacher Exams to get the state teacher's certificate.

The NTE test reminded me of the SAT, which I had done poorly on in high school, and I was really afraid that I would not do well. However, I did pass the test, and doing so made me proud. I was convinced that I had passed the NTE because of my life experiences. This was the only reason that I could come up with, because some twenty years before I had failed the same type of test.

After about six months, I went back to Washington, D.C., to visit with Brenda and Dwayne. I was very much in love with Brenda and very concerned about how Dwayne was doing. On that visit I had a talk with Dwayne that changed both of our lives. I said to him, "I'm going to ask you again, Dwayne; do you want to be a star and make something out of your life?" He said he did, so I told him to come live in Newport News and stay with his grandmother, and I would help change his life. I talked with Brenda and she agreed that both of them wanted to relocate back home. She said, "I need a change in my life and Dwayne needs to change his attitude and do better in school. I want him to make something out of his life and I believe you can help give him the guidance he needs." I was really encouraged after that visit with Brenda and Dwayne. The first thought I had was that I could get to know Brenda better and maybe we could develop a relationship that would lead to starting a family. Second, I was prepared to help Dwayne get his future together. I thought it would be great to teach and coach him.

One afternoon, on the job as a security officer at an apartment complex, I watched a girls' softball game on the complex's baseball field. I was in my security uniform—not exactly hiding, but not wanting to be caught in my uniform, either—standing behind a large trash chute. I heard a voice and saw my old friend Dixon. I was glad to see him, but I felt ashamed that he should see me in a security uniform. He walked up to me and said, "I heard you were back in town. Why haven't you come see me?"

"Dixon, it's a long story . . ." I started.

We talked for a while about my return home, and he said, "Tommy, why don't you use that recreation degree you have and come work with me for the city's Parks and Recreation Department?" I said, "Dixon, I want to be a teacher and football coach, but if you can get me a part-time job working with you, I would love that. "

"It's a done deal; just come see me."

Well, I did go see him, and I have been working part-time for the city of Newport News Parks and Recreation Department ever since.

I began my teaching career at Menchville High School as a special education teacher and assistant football coach under the legendary football and track coach Charlie Nuttycombe. I was very excited to learn from people like him in my new career. I was a new teacher, and I wanted to earn respect by working hard and learning how things were done. However, the transition would not be an easy one.

There were coworkers who had preconceived ideas about me and my abilities based on my background as a professional football player and movie actor. There were also those who thought that I got the teaching job because of my name. I began to feel the jealousy and resentment real fast. The first time I met my teacher mentor, she introduced herself and said she had graduated from Clemson University. Her first comment to me was that during her college days she'd observed that football players would get a lot of privileges that regular students didn't get. I did not respond; I just looked at her and smiled.

I felt that she was trying to put me down. I could tell that she really did not believe I was qualified for my position. That conversation set a negative tone for our relationship. She asked me, "Mr. Reamon, could you have worked in Parks and Recreation to help kids?" referring to my undergraduate degree in Recreation. I said very nicely, "No, because I want to be a part of their academic learning experience, and I put the time and effort into earning a graduate certification to enable me to do so." Nevertheless, she acted as if I was in the wrong place.

I was the only male in Special Education with Learning Disabilities in the four high schools in our city—it is not a field that attracts many men. I would come to learn that the demands of this field of teaching would also require a lot of paperwork.

This is one part of the job I did not like. I enjoyed my relationship with the kids, and I gained much respect for the individualized teaching approach I used. I use many similar approaches today in coaching. Just as in athletics, in Special Education, the key is to find out what motivates students based on their limitations and help them to reach their maximum potential. In the best-case scenario, you can motivate an athlete to perform above his or her capabilities.

My first football coaching experience was also at Menchville High School. Coach Nuttycombe was a great organizer, and he assigned me to certain duties for the players. I coached the quarterbacks, running backs, and wide receivers on the varsity team. One of my duties was to communicate with college coaches about the players I thought could go on to play college football. He showed courage in utilizing my talents in this way. I had contacts with college coaches around the country, especially in the Kansas junior colleges. The junior college contacts were very important since many of the student athletes were nonqualifiers under NCAA requirements because of low grades and SAT scores. I knew from experience how the junior college route would benefit those kinds of kids if they were interested in going to college.

In my first two football seasons as an assistant coach, I coached a unique group of talented student athletes that included my new stepson, Dwayne Knight. Dwayne's mother and I had gotten married in August, just before the start of football season. She would stay in Washington, D. C., and complete her job contract, and would join us by the holidays in December. Dwayne stayed with his grandmother and attended school with me. He was entering the tenth grade, but I wanted him to repeat the ninth grade. That way he could start over fresh, have a chance to adjust, and I could work with his football development. During his first two years, he played linebacker and wide receiver. He was doing better in school, but he began to hang out with the wrong crowd of kids. He showed great promise to be a college scholarship athlete and I was not about to let him destroy the dreams that we had agreed on.

In Dwayne's senior year at Menchville, we decided to take him out of that school and send him to a private school. I was convinced this was the best decision for his future. The plan was for him to attend Nansemond Suffolk Academy. The school was located forty minutes from our home. He would be the only black athlete in any sport at the school. This was a bold decision on our part, but the goal was for him to improve his grades, do well enough on the SAT, and earn a football scholarship. At the same time, I decided to accept the head football coaching position at Manor High School in Portsmouth, Virginia. Since my commute to work each morning took me very close to Dwayne's school, we drove together. We spent some quality time together on those rides across the James River Bridge every morning for a year. I felt very close to him, and I began to love him. I admired Dwayne for sacrificing his senior year and the things that were important to any young student in his last year of high school. Giving up the social life with his peers to commit to getting a scholarship showed he had character. He played every position on their football team and was voted the most valuable player

At the new school he was selected to the Virginia Independent Schools All-State team, and he was recruited by James Madison, Missouri, and Virginia Tech. The recruiting coach from Virginia Tech, Keith Jones did a super job. Dwayne signed a scholarship to attend there, and played for four years. After he finished Virginia Tech, he came back home to work with me as an assistant coach at Ferguson High School. I had always told Dwayne that he would be a great coach, and he was.

Once Dwayne told me about a comment that ninth-grader Michael Vick had made to him. He said, "I was driving Michael home after a football practice and as we were approaching his apartment complex Vick said, 'Coach Knight, one day I'm going to get out of this neighborhood.'" Dwayne told him to stick with Coach Reamon if he wanted to make good on that dream. After one year as a coach, Dwayne tried out for the Winnipeg Blueboomers of the Canadian Football League, and he played in that league for five years.

The other great football players on Menchville High School's varsity and junior varsity teams were Kwamie Lassiter (Kansas Junior College/University of Kansas/Arizona Cardinals), Antonio Banks (Virginia Tech/Minnesota Vikings), Shawn Hamlet (Florida State), Fred Lassiter (Virginia Tech), and Dion Johnson (Kansas Junior College/East Carolina/Houston Oilers).

Each one of these young and talented athletes had unique personal situations, like all students. However, I could see myself in these players and their need for a personal relationship with me as their coach, and I was often overwhelmed by the players as they sought guidance and direction from me. I learned very fast that high school coaching is about relationships, and I began to see a bigger picture form as I worked with these student athletes. I also began to see the critical role that I would have to play in their lives if they were going to have a chance to be successful.

As I observed each player, I thought of my own experiences, and what I had I learned as a result of my ambitions. Education is the key to getting out and staying out of generational poverty.

I didn't have the resources that young people have today. What I didn't know, I had to figure out on my own. I transported myself from the inner city to junior college and beyond by sheer willpower. Today, with all the state- and federally funded programs in schools to help lift children from poverty, there's no excuse for not knowing about the importance of an education. Success is not the big mystery it used to be. However, we do so much for kids now; sometimes I think we do too much.

Are we any more successful at helping them to be independent thinkers, or are we just protecting them from adverse consequences? I try hard to focus on the ones who want to make something of themselves, but I can't help but feel sadness for those who just sit back and wait for us to pass them along. So many abuse the goodwill of the system, rather than use its generosity and concern to help them in their independent growth. I try to combat the "take it for granted" attitude that so many kids bring to my program.

In my system, students are encouraged to pursue other interests in addition to football. I tell them that they must focus on an academic or vocational endeavor, depending on their abilities and inclinations. For instance, many of my former players are highly successful as firemen, police officers, plumbers, and so on. I constantly refer to them, as well as to pro athletes, as success stories who came out of my program. I tell my players that being prepared isn't just about making more money, but about being good at what you do and loving your work. I want my players to be able to walk out of the projects and into an upscale neighborhood and be well received, to rise above cultural barriers. One key to that is listening to what the other side has to say.

The minority students in my program will often ask, "Isn't that 'acting white'?" I tell them that success has no color. That doesn't mean letting go of your heritage, but it does mean acknowledging that other cultures have ideas and that we can learn from all cultures. I call it navigation. When a boat captain is good, he can navigate in all kinds of waters. Minority students and athletes must learn how to navigate between and across cultures.

People can leave poverty when they have a goal or vision of something they want to be or have; when they are in a situation that is so painful that anything would be better; when they have someone like me, a mentor or role model, to show them a different way or convince them that they *could* live differently; or when they possess a specific talent or ability that provides an opportunity. Often a student who has been in a deprived home environment will ask me how I made the journey out. My answer is that it has to do with a relationship with a teacher, counselor, or a coach like myself who makes a suggestion or takes an interest in them as individuals.

I had to listen to and trust people outside my culture, something so many of today's kids are unwilling to do. Sure, sometimes I placed too much trust in other people, but today I see kids who aren't willing to trust anyone—and too often, parents aren't helping them with that. In fact, sometimes I think that, with the examples they set, parents teach their kids to have poor attitudes. For instance, when a kid sees his parent go off on an innocent sales clerk over the price of an item in a department store, what message does he get? That it's okay to sound off, display an attitude, at the slightest provocation? What message does it send a kid when his parent blows up with road rage?

I've actually had kids tell me that their parents told them not to take any crap off anyone, especially teachers. With this kind of advice, how will their children learn to trust or respect adults in authority? That is where good teachers and counselors must bridge the gap between the poor examples kids see at home and the winning attitudes they will need to display if they are to be successful.

Sometimes it's a matter of helping them bridge cultural gaps, as I've said. For instance, when a black player comes to me complaining about how hard a certain white teacher is, I ask him if he or she is any harder than I am. If the kid says yes, then I say, "Well, I'll make amends in practice today." Sometimes I visit that so-called hard teacher and thank her for challenging my player, and let her know that my player will not only meet the challenge, he will do so respectfully. I also encourage my players to thank their teachers for all their help. These are the early lessons in human relations that I want them to learn.

I have tried to create relationships with players because everything always begins as one person to another. The question that I tangle with a lot as a relationship coach is, what exactly is meant by a "relationship"? I ask myself plenty of times, "Should the player become my personal friend?" The answer to this question for me is yes. I feel this emotional tie to my players all the time.

I know that perhaps not everyone is prepared to become so personally involved, but it's the only real answer I have to why I've been successful. My success has nothing to do with winning state championships; it is about my firm belief that all of these kids we are entrusted with have the ability to shine and sparkle like the diamonds they are.

Have you ever seen a diamond before it is cut and polished? Underneath that ugly, flat blackness something special hides, awaiting the chance to shine. It is not until the diamond is placed in the skilled hands of a diamond cutter that its beauty and brilliance emerge. Every child is like a diamond, each with his or her own special brilliance.

Every child just needs the chance to discover what he or she can do, and then be given the necessary support to obtain his or her dream. I feel it is my responsibility to see that every child has the chance and the tools he or she needs. If I can provide those, then I consider myself a success.

I ask myself if there are boundaries to the relationships. Absolutely. However, when I am faced with the right situation, like I was with the rough diamonds I talk about in this book, I feel in my heart that I was sent to guide their futures.

In my years as a teacher I have seen these young men everywhere, and I want to take them all and make them shine. However, I have accepted that it is impossible to embrace them all, and have learned, instead, to take the talents God gave me and use them to help those I can. Simply put, I am a football player; it is what I do best. So I have used that talent to develop those few diamonds that I am blessed to be able to coach. Occasionally a student comes along who reminds me of myself when I was younger. He may have a special talent, a great love for the game, a great drive to be the best, or he may just fill me with joy to watch as he plays. Every once in a while I get very lucky and am given a student who possesses all those qualities. When I realize such a diamond is in my presence, I can only compare the feeling to the experience of falling in love at first sight. I just know this one is special. Something in him just speaks to me: he wants to be the best, he needs to be the best, he feeds on success, and I am driven to help him succeed. We all have the ability to develop talent in athletes like these; it just takes time and patience, tempered with a sense of urgency.

Rough Diamonds

The year of my first head coaching position, I knew that I had the qualities to be a successful coach. Like most coaches, I learned my techniques from the coaches and players I have known during their careers. I would take the best from these people I had been around to help make me a coach, but I was prepared to build a program my own way. The areas that I think were important then and are a trademark of my program today are:

- being well organized and using my time wisely
- being the best teacher in the system
- showing loyalty to my players and staff
- developing a solid work ethic, taking the time to do the job well regardless of how long it takes
- observing professionalism in all things I do
- requiring integrity on the part of all my players
- respecting my players, staff, and anyone I work with
- building confidence and patience
- building team unity—"we before I"
- demanding accountability to God, administration, players, and coaching staff

When I talk about how I built my high school football programs at Manor in Portsmouth, at Ferguson, and presently at Warwick, in Newport News, Virginia, I do not speak of Xs and Os of the game. Football is very simple in its basic principles, and I assume that most coaches and fans are thoroughly familiar with the Xs and Os. I like to talk about concepts and philosophies that have been a strong influence in my programs' success. I measure my success by the success of the individual student athlete. I can speak as a coach on the complexities of preparation, organization, motivation, and discipline, and it can help coaches get from hoping they can win to believing they *should* win. I have found that if I promote an atmosphere of enthusiasm within the program, encourage creativity, and stimulate motivation, then team spirit is solidified and the team is stronger.

But like most high school football programs, mine has never been blessed with an abundance of football talent on a yearly basis, so I have had to search for ways to produce a solid, consistent program while highlighting individual players.

The key for me in building a football program lies in my ability to judge people and situations, to decide whom I can place trust in. Doing this well requires a high degree of self-evaluation and honesty. I have to be careful. I try to live up to the image I project, that I want to see. It is a human failing to perceive only our strengths and assets and none of our weaknesses and liabilities. Like most people, I find it difficult to acknowledge my own shortcomings, but I have found that self-delusion and failure to perceive shortcomings will most certainly work to my detriment, and can overshadow otherwise excellent job skills and performances. Therefore, I take stock of myself and do a self-appraisal. I do not delude myself that I have all the answers and can learn nothing new. I explain it this way. I have an image that I want others to see in me. I am always working on my personal character traits, and I constantly evaluate my management skills to make sure that the image I project is genuine. At the same time, I try to keep that image realistic and make sure I don't project traits I do not possess and come off like a phony.

It has been critical for me that I be perceived as a role model. My credibility as a head coach has always depended on how I conduct myself—on what I do, rather than simply on the things that I say. I have had to bring out the best of my behavior and couple it with my celebrity background. The players, the administrators, the faculty, and my staff all have evaluated my behavior, and they know quickly if I am the kind of person who practices what I preach. With that in mind, I learned early in my coaching career simply that I had better practice what I preach. If not, how can I teach character development to the student athletes in my program? When I talk like this about coaching, many of my friends say that I must think I am a psychologist.

Most of my coaching career has been centered on developing relationships with my players. Obviously, I have had some talented players, but for a team to be as good as it can be, they have to buy into what I as the coach am doing. All the players have to feel that I am a part of them and they are a part of me. I have cultivated that technique to some degree, but continue to refine the psychology. What you will read about Aaron Brooks and Michael Vick may convince you that a little training in psychology could be an important ingredient in the success of any team. Because these two players and others have believed what I told them, they got beyond high school and college, then into the NFL as top professionals

Throughout my coaching career I have been determined to find student athletes who would buy into my idea of goal-planning. To me, goal-planning is as crucial to success as scoring more points than your opponent is to victory. A leader in anything must learn how to plan properly to reach his or her goals, and how to motivate a team or himself to strive for them. The most excitement I can get in my profession is when I hear an individual student athlete say, "Coach, I want to be a star." Boy, do I get pumped up. We get right to work planning goals. I have five elements that are the foundation of goal planning: desire, imagination, courage, confidence, and knowledge.

Desire is the product of the fusion of passion and will. It is the embryo from which all ideals emerge, the catalyst that turns existing knowledge into new discovery, dreams into reality, and ideas into action. I have said many times, "My football program consists of ath-letes who are dreamers." Nothing of value has ever been accomplished without passion, without desire.

Imagination is the ability to break through the mental and emo-tional restrictions placed on you by your background. It consists of a flow of concepts, ideas, and knowledge that allows you to envision possibilities, and in doing so develop a plan of action that works toward achievement. Without imagination, little can be accomplished.

Courage is not, as some would have you believe, a lack of fear. It is the ability to overcome fear and to act rationally in the face of it. To be courageous you must first develop tough mental discipline and moral character. In order to act with courage, you must be steadfast in your beliefs and goals, regardless of outside threats and pressures.

Confidence allows you to believe in your ability. It stems from a positive mental attitude, a strong desire, a vivid imagination, and unflinching courage. Confidence allows you to maintain your direction in the face of doubts and ridicule and to remain undeterred by other people's negative attitudes. It is the element that securely bonds a leader and his team as they work toward mutual goals.

Knowledge is a properly balanced blend of information (or facts) and practical experience. In order to work toward a goal you must first fully understand the value of that goal and what is necessary to achieve it. You should be certain that the goals you select are attainable, within the scope of your circumstances, and that you possess sufficient knowledge to achieve them.

Although no plan is perfect, and some may not work out to your every expectation, a plan must be put into place. Its enactment and refinement will determine who wins, who is successful, and who benefits. In the next chapters you will see how goal planning was instrumental in the careers of Aaron Brooks and Michael Vick. These chapters will answer the questions about how they got to the pros, how they emerged from their low-income neighborhoods, how they survived as students, and who helped them along the way.

I look back on those years when I started coaching as very important in my life, but I remember 1989 in particular as a banner year in my life. First of all, right after the Christmas break, I accepted my first head coaching position at Manor High School. Then, on August 12, a second event fulfilled a lifelong dream. I was finally a father with the birth of Tommy Jr. It was a rainy Saturday morning, which forced us to have practice inside the school's gymnasium. I'd had no indication from Brenda that morning that my "Second Heartbeat," as I refer to Tommy Jr., was about to enter the world.

We were practicing on the gym floor, running through drills, when one of the coaches heard knocking on the doors. He answered it and motioned me over. As I approached, I heard a police radio, and my first thought was that something had happened to Brenda and the baby. Practice had started the week before, and even before that I had been preparing for the season. Because I had not been able to be home with her, she had been doing a lot of the preparations for the baby on her own. In fact, that morning I had left the house very early and in a rush. Brenda had been up before me and was busy cleaning the bathroom. She hadn't stopped as I left, but had called out to say goodbye just as I was leaving. Driving to school that morning, I thought about her and how strange it seemed that she was up that early cleaning the bathroom, but soon I forgot about it as I settled in to practice. Then, as the policeman approached, the fear that something had happened squeezed my heart.

He informed me that my mother called the Portsmouth police department and told them who I was and said my wife was in labor.

He said, "Coach, it's rainy out there. Please be careful driving to the hospital." He paused, then asked "Where do you have to go?" I told him I had to get to Newport News; and he said, "Well, Coach, I am not supposed to do this, but under the circumstances, I will escort you to the James River Bridge, then you can handle it from there." I thanked him nervously. I didn't realize I had been holding my breath, but now it came out in a big sigh of relief. My thoughts raced ahead almost as fast as I was driving. Brenda was in labor, and I was about to become a father. I couldn't suppress my joy.

We drove to the bridge together, and this was the first time I had ever driven that fast without worrying about the police or getting a speeding ticket; this day I would have them on my side.

I arrived at the hospital and waited through about two hours of labor. At eleven o'clock, I was handed a baby boy. As with all small babies, I had this nagging fear that I would drop him because he reminded me of a football. I kept thinking how I do have a history of fumbling the football and I did not want to fumble him out of my arms.

I had wanted to be father for a long time, but now I wondered how I'd be as a daddy. Of course, I worried about the timing. Because the football season had just started, I would miss many of the important early weeks with Tommy Jr. Leaving at five in the morning and not getting home until eight or nine at night is not exactly the best way to be a good father. Even when I was home, I often worked until eleven or twelve o'clock at night. When would I have time to spend with the baby and my wife? During my years as a professional football player and in Hollywood, I had been single with no one to consider except myself, but now with a family I had to think of others. I was anxious but excited, and we made it all work out.

Tommy Jr., age four.

Coach Reamon and Kwamie smiling for the camera at a recent summer camp.

7. Kwamie Lassiter

The Lassiter brothers lived with their grandmother when I first met them. She was the pillar of strength in the Lassiters' large family of children. Very few kids and grandmothers have been as devoted to one another as they were to her and she was to them. She was a tremendous influence on their lives, but only because they allowed her to be. They knew that their grandmother wanted what was best for them. She was always a big supporter of anything I did for them. Kwamie was the oldest, and he inherited his grandmother's strength and character. He told me many times in school that he wanted to play big-time college football. He was so polite and quiet, and demonstrated a seriousness about life not often seen in others his age. He is also one of the most genuinely caring people I've ever met.

Kwamie had, like all great leaders on a team, a wonderful combination of toughness and intelligence. Nothing came easily for him. He had to earn everything.

In his junior year, he injured his knee and had to have surgery to repair damage to the ligaments. He did not have medical insurance. I talked with a Dr. Phillip Powell, who agreed to perform the surgery, and I signed the papers for him to have the surgery done.

However, with all his strengths, Kwamie had poor grades. He asked me to help him get into college. I saw myself in him. I could think back some twenty years and recall that I'd had the same problems he was now faced with. I wanted to do whatever I could to help him reach his dreams. He had low grades and a low SAT score and did not qualify for an NCAA athletic scholarship, so I helped him get accepted at Butler Community College in Kansas. There he had a great playing career and was named to various All-American teams. He improved as a student athlete and as a person. For Kwamie, the Kansas junior college experience was a stepping stone to where he wanted to go. It was tough adjusting to the environment and being an inner-city kid from the South. In his second year at Butler JC, I visited my own junior college in Fort Scott, Kansas, where I was inducted into the Fort Scott Junior College Hall of Fame. Kwamie traveled from nearby Butler County to attend the ceremony. When I saw him in that environment and watched how he handled himself with people, I witnessed one of my children grown from a boy to a young man. He said to me on that visit in Kansas, "Coach, this was the best decision I could have made to get my life together and have a second chance at reaching my goals, but I want to come closer to home—if possible, to Virginia Tech."

I responded, "Kwamie, when that time comes to transfer, I will try to help get you closer to home." After two junior college All-American seasons, Kwamie and I talked about him transferring to a Division One school near home.

He signed a football scholarship to attend Virginia Tech, graduated from Butler County Community College, and was home for the summer. Then, that summer he was notified by the Virginia Tech admissions office that he would not be admitted to their school because he lacked some of the required core courses.

We talked with everyone connected to this problem and could not find a solution. I asked him if he wanted me to contact another school that would admit him. He said no. So we asked the Virginia Tech coaches to honor his scholarship for the second semester, and they agreed. Kwamie enrolled in Thomas Nelson Community College near his home, and volunteered as my assistant football coach. In addition, he needed money to live, so he found a night job working with my sister Willie at Fort Eustis Military Hospital as a records and file clerk.

He was so determined to do all the right things. He worked and took the two core courses he needed to be admitted into Virginia Tech. Kwamie came to see me at the end of the first semester at Thomas Nelson, during the Christmas holidays. He had bad news. He had received a D in his Algebra II class, so now, for the second time, he would not be admitted. We talked about other schools that had shown an interest in him after his junior college days. I called the University of Kansas for him. They were still interested, but the new semester had just started and he would have to leave for Kansas immediately. He did.

Kwamie had a super first season for the Kansas Jayhawks, and in that 1993 season he was named by *Sports Illustrated* as the defensive player of the week for his performance against Oklahoma State University. He had 2 interceptions, 1 forced fumble, 2 pass deflections, and 11 tackles. He called me to say that I was not the only one who made the *Sports Illustrated* player of the week award. He was teasing me because of stories I once told him of my performance against the University of Colorado of the Big Eight Conference, a performance that earned me the same recognition by the same magazine. He was fulfilling his dreams. He told me that his high school girlfriend, Ericka, was living with him. He said, "Coach, she is very supportive and has always believed in my dreams. She and I often talk about your stories about how caring and personable the people are in the Midwest. They really are. It's been great."

During his second year, he suffered a broken collarbone in the second game. The coaches contacted me, and we talked about the semester he had spent out of school. The reason they were interested in this was that they were going to request a medical redshirt year from the NCAA. A medical redshirt is used to allow an extra full season of eligibility for an athlete who has been injured early in the year and missed most of the season. However, Kwamie's case not only involved the collarbone injury but was complicated by whether he would be able to play if he transferred to Virginia Tech, which was still his goal. He felt devastated by this situation because he was beginning to adjust to a major college program with success.

The NCAA denied his first request for the medical redshirt year, and the University of Kansas football program hired an attorney to argue his case. After many depositions submitted by the Virginia Tech football coaches and myself, the attorney's investigation in Kwamie's case found special circumstances regarding the semester spent out of school. The NCAA reversed its ruling on the decision to let him play his last year at Kansas. I remember telling the coach at Kansas, "Kwamie will be the best player on your team not because of athletic ability, but because of character and loyalty." He earned second team All-Big Eight Conference honors in 1994 with 44 tackles, 32 assisted tackles, and 3 interceptions.

Kwamie was not drafted into the NFL; instead, he was a free agent selection by the Arizona Cardinals, and he was a long shot to make the team under head coach Buddy Ryan. He did, however, make the team as a special teams player, but after five games he suffered a broken ankle during practice. We talked afterward. He was very concerned about his future with the Cardinals. I told him again that he should keep his head up and try to do everything the team management asked of him. Because the team was not winning games that season, Buddy Ryan was fired at the end of the season. A new head coach, Vince Tobin, was hired, and he knew little about Kwamie. In fact, one reason Kwamie was buried on the depth chart in 1996 was that the coaches weren't sure if he played corner back or safety. Kwamie said to me then, "All they had to do was put me at one or the other, and I would make plays." Although the new coaches did not know Kwamie, I knew Coach Tobin. He had coached me at the University of Missouri. I called him and talked about Kwamie as a person and told him he had played for me in high school. Coach Tobin and I talked on three different occasions regarding Kwamie's performances and talents. In one of the talks he said, "Kwamie has had to overcome a lot of odds to get here, and he doesn't complain. Tommy, to be honest with you, he will make the team as a backup free safety, a nickel defensive back, and he will perform on our special teams." I was so proud to be involved with his professional career, and I was very thankful to Coach Tobin.

For the first few years, Kwamie was a "blue collar worker" for the Arizona Cardinals team. He was serious and had a great attitude, and it was reflected in his play. His teammates complimented him all the time.

They said things like, "Kwamie is always around the ball. He happens to be there when the ball is tipped or overthrown." In the 1997 season, he played a key role as the team's nickel back. The nickel back is the best available defensive back to help defend against a passing offense. In addition, he was the most outstanding special teams player. We visited with each other annually when the Cardinals came to play in Washington against the Redskins. I felt special, sitting in the stands watching my rough diamond perform. He always invited me to the locker room after the game to talk before heading back to Arizona. He called in 1998 when he was promoted to the starting role at free safety in place of Pat Tillman against the Kansas City Chiefs. I thought it was great for him to get the starting job in Kansas, where he'd played college football, and I teased him on the phone the night before the game. I told him that I had sent the entire states of Missouri and Kansas to cheer him on during the game. I was sentimental about his first NFL game being at my former professional team's stadium and in the state where I had played college football.

Kwamie had a dream season. He was the top defensive back for the Cardinals with 9 combined tackles for a 19-17 win over the New Orleans Saints. He closed out the regular season in grand style with one interception on San Diego Charger passer Craig Whelihan in each quarter. Those interceptions marked the first time since 1985 that a player intercepted 4 passes in one game. He completed the season with excellent performances against Dallas in a wild card playoff win and in the divisional playoff loss to Minnesota. His best year was 2001, a breakout season with a team best and career-high 100 solo tackles and 9 interceptions as a Pro Bowl alternate. His interception total ranked second in the NFC, and he was named NFC defensive player of the month for November. He has started every game for the past three seasons and added 453 tackles and 12 interceptions in that span of time. He owns a stretch of 94 consecutive games entering the 2002 season, and has been a franchise player since his incredible 2001 season. A franchise player tag on your back means that your team needs you and respects you. In the world of the NFL, it also means that it's time to negotiate a new contract. Kwamie now lives in

Phoenix, Arizona, in the off-season with his wife Ericka, his high-school girlfriend, who supported his career from high school to junior college to the University of Kansas up to today—along with their four sons. Erika sends me a yearly Christmas card, and is a wonderful woman.

I always told Kwamie, "When you make it to the NFL, give some of your time back to the community." So, in May of 1999, I was happy to hear that he and Ericka had established the Lassiters' T.A.C.K.L.E. (Teaching All Children to Kickoff Leadership through Education) Foundation. Kwamie said, "Coach, we are trying to do what you told us to do." The foundation was started because they did not want children to be exposed to the same economic hardships that they had dealt with in schools as youths. Through this organization the Lassiters seek to motivate and promote the success of children through education. This task can only be accomplished by combating those factors that distract them from their education. Kwamie said, "Children should not have to worry about where they are going to get school supplies and books. Their only focus should be learning." With that in mind, Kwamie and Ericka provide schools with supplies for the underprivileged. They established the T.A.C.K.L.E. Book Scholarship, which pays for a full year of books for a college-bound high school student. This was very important to Ericka. She recalls having to go to the library at Norfolk State University to copy chapters of her course books because she couldn't afford all her books each semester.

Kwamie told me about how T.A.C.K.L.E. adopted a local elementary school in Phoenix, Arizona. That school, like so many others, lacked essential resources, so the T.A.C.K.L.E. staff, which consists of Kwamie, Ericka, her sister, Lydia, and a friend, Ronette, meet with teachers after school, listen to their needs, and shop for sponsorship in addition to providing books and supplies. When their organization delivers the materials to the school, they are overwhelmed with thank you notes from grateful students and teachers.

Their foundation also hosts many events each year that involve children and working in the community. As an incentive for children to remain focused in school, they sponsor several children to attend Arizona Cardinals home football games. For many of these kids, getting tickets is a once-in-a-lifetime opportunity.

Just recently, Kwamie called me for some advice on how to run a football camp. He made me feel very special when he said, "Coach, I'm taking a page from your book of memories and starting a football camp in the Phoenix area." His reasons for starting the camp sounded similar to the ones I had thirty years before. His free annual camp allows boys and girls an opportunity to learn the principles of football and meet current and former NFL players. At the camp, they teach the importance of hard work and dedication. Both Kwamie and Ericka work hard as a team on all the foundation's projects, and they love the children. I have heard Kwamie say many times that giving back to the community and children is "no longer a choice but a must." I'm so very proud of this rough diamond.

Lassiter family Christmas card photo.

Rough Diamonds

In 1987, When Kwamie was about to start at Butler County Junior College in Kansas, I drove him to the airport to catch his flight. While we waited before he could board the plane, we talked about his plans for the future and about his brother, Fred. Kwamie was very concerned about leaving him. He wanted Fred to have an easier path as a student athlete. He said, "Coach, I need a big favor from you. If you do this for me, I will never forget it. He needs your guidance and help. I don't want him to make the same academic mistakes that I did. They hurt my chances to get into a major college football program, and I don't want the same thing to happen to Fred. Please take care of him in your special way, the way you did me."

I replied, "I will take care of him as if he were my own. Don't you worry; you just go out to Kansas and do your best. Better yet, do what I did out there years ago. Leave Fred to me." Thus, Fred and I developed a very special relationship in the months to come. However, I did not realize just how involved in his development I would become.

Kwamie's request would not be the last one like it. Michael Vick recently made a similar request regarding his brother Marcus. Because Kwamie and Michael had such a great influence on their younger brothers, both Fred and Marcus worshiped the ground their older brothers walked on.

After Kwamie graduated, I would spend one more semester at Menchville High School in Newport News as a Special Education teacher and assistant football coach. I enjoyed teaching, but I wanted to be a head football coach. A former World Football League coach, Dwayne Jeter, was assistant principal at Manor High School in the nearby city of Portsmouth. He contacted me about his school's search for a football coach. I interviewed for the job and accepted it. I resigned at Menchville at the end of the first semester. After the Christmas holiday break I reported to Manor High School and began teaching Special Education classes at one of their middle schools.

Over that same holiday break, Fred Lassiter's life began to change. He was a sophomore and a football player at Menchville. Because his brother and best friend, Kwamie, had just left for college in Kansas, he moved in with his mother after years of living with his grandmother.

After this move, I got a call from Fred almost every night for a month. We talked about the important events in his life, and I knew by the sound of his voice that he was depressed about living with his mother. He told me that she had plans to marry a friend in the military and relocate to North Carolina. She wanted Fred to move with her, and naturally he did not want to go.

I try very hard to stay out of the family matters of my players, but sometimes my heart just takes over when they are faced with some of the issues they have to deal with. But family matter or not, I always try to help my players with whatever issues they may be facing, so when Fred told me that he didn't want to go with his mother and disrupt his life so much, I first told him that such a move could help him experience a family life with his mother and stepfather. I immediately thought of the excitement I had as a youth when my mother had remarried, hoping to make life better for my brother, my sister, and me. The adjustments we all had to make in order to live comfortably did change my life. Because my situation had been so similar to Fred's, I felt a lot of sympathy for him. However, I had established a very strong relationship with all of his family, especially his grandmother.

Kwamie and his grandmother then asked if Fred could come and live with me. This was a monumental request, but I had promised Kwamie that I would help Fred. His grandmother felt that Fred might not get the right guidance in a new location that far from home. She had seen the impact I had made on Kwamie's life and wanted the same for Fred. I was troubled by this request, only because I knew it might cause hardship in my own family, and later it did. But I wanted to help Fred any way I could.

I asked my wife, Brenda, what she thought about the idea. She said, "It would be hard on us, but do what you have to do." I replied, "Brenda, he needs my help." I felt she allowed me to do this only because she had made the same request of me to help her son, Dwayne.

I was given parental custody of Fred, and he attended Manor High with me. I spent a lot of time nursing him on attitude and behavior. He was a very quiet person, and had a smile so big that you could fall in love with him. As an athlete, he was a raw talent. He could play with the best and was very intelligent and knowledgeable about football. I once said, "Fred Lassiter might have been the best athletic quarterback that I ever coached." At six-foot-three, he was slim like Aaron Brooks and as athletic as Michael or Marcus Vick. While playing at Manor High School, he was considered one of the best quarterbacks on the East Coast. However, he was competing against another great athletic quarterback, Aaron Sparrow of Woodrow Wilson High School, also in Portsmouth. Sparrow and his coach, Darnell Moore, won two Virginia state championships in three years. When I think about this today, I realize that three of my great players—Fred, Aaron, and Michael—all competed against equally great players who lived either within blocks of them or no more than a few miles away. Nevertheless, all three became national high school recruits and experienced the ultimate in media exposure. They all had an opportunity to showcase their talents, regardless of the successes of their rivals.

Yet no matter how brightly Fred shined, he could not stand to be considered second to Aaron Sparrow. His obstinancy about this caused me great frustration. He would often criticize his situation and team-mates, and of course, I chastised him for his negative behavior. I tried to make him see that his team was the best supporting cast he had. Sparrow just had a better supporting cast. I wanted him to accept that fact and appreciate his strengths.

He once said to me, "Coach, I have always been second in my life, with my grandma and mother, second to Kwamie—"

I fired back, "Maybe so, but you can't cry about that or feel like nobody recognizes what you have done. As long as you know you have done your best, then it's not important what people think of you. You are one of the best football players in the country. Be appreciative of that fact, and learn to be humble."

Fred spent one year at Virginia Tech. He started the school year as a redshirt freshman on the football team. As with Aaron Brooks and later Michael Vick, I thought it best that he not play his first year;

instead, he should take time to adjust to the demands of college academics and football. His recruiting coach, Keith Jones, was a personal-relationship coach like me, and he helped Fred navigate the tricky currents of college life. Coach Jones had done a great job helping my stepson, Dwayne, adjust to college life when he arrived at Virginia Tech as a freshman. I felt comfortable that Fred had a great supporting staff surrounding him and would do well. Unfortunately, that was not the case.

He could not adjust to the academic demands. Even with tutoring sessions at night to help, he would not apply himself, and therefore, he failed to achieve. During the spring football practice he became a serious contender for the starting quarterback position. He competed against another talented player named Maurice Deshazo. I have said to Frank Beamer, Tech's head coach, that if Fred Lassiter had stuck it out in school, Tech football fans might have cheered him instead of Deshazo.

That summer Fred disappeared from school. I received calls from the football coaches that Fred was to report to summer school. He was required to take two classes to be eligible to play football the upcoming season. I contacted every conceivable relative and friend of Fred's, but no one knew where he was. Two weeks later, his grandmother called me to say that he was in Portsmouth. She said, "Coach, he got a girlfriend pregnant and he will not return to college."

By that time I had accepted a new job as head football coach at Ferguson High School back in Newport News, and was excited about starting a new program. I did not hear from Fred Lassiter. I did not know where he was or what he was doing with his life. The way he quit school without saying goodbye disappointed me tremendously. I felt betrayed and hurt. I realized after some time passed that he could not display the maturity that I worked so hard to help him develop.

Months later, during the half time of one of my games at Ferguson High School, I was walking off the field with Aaron Brooks, my quarterback at the time, when Fred Lassiter stepped in front of me and flashed that smile that I had cherished from the first time I met him. I was so shocked and overjoyed to see him that I temporarily forgot my football team in the locker room waiting for me. I hugged him and told him that I missed him.

He replied, "I miss you too, Coach; when you get some time, could we talk?" I told him I would be glad to; however, I didn't talk with him again until late November after my football season was over. He came by the school to tell me he was sorry that he let me down. He said, "I just didn't want the dream as much as you wanted it for me. I was ashamed and embarrassed to face you. I knew I let you down." He continued by blaming his failures on not being a good student. I told him that I had not been a good student either, but I had worked hard enough to at least finish college. I told him how sad it made me that he felt he could not talk to me about his struggles with school. However, I reminded him then and repeated again my concern that he needed more education. It didn't have to be academic; why not try a technical degree or training? I told him I didn't care then and don't care today if he never played football as long as he got more education and training so he could have a chance at being successful in life. It would be even more critical now that he had a son.

We talked more and I asked him if he had any plans. He said, "Coach, that's why I've come to see you. I want to know if you can help me get in college somewhere." I responded, "Are you sure that is what you want to do now?" He said, "Yes." I told him I'd work on trying to get him into a smaller college; he could become a student again and still have a chance to play football. I found a school, Elizabeth City State University in North Carolina, and worked out all the arrangements to get him admitted and receive money from football scholarships. He was to report to college for the second semester. I took off work with my son, Tommy Jr., to take Fred to ECSU. During the two-hour drive I remember asking Fred if he would stay in school. He said, "Coach, I'm going to make this work."

Two weeks later the football coaches called me to say that Fred had left school. I tried to contact him again. Frustrated beyond tolerance, I began to face the truth about Fred: You can lead the horse to water but you can't make him drink. He was the first player that I had invested so much of my personal life in, and even though I developed a solid relationship with him, I somehow felt personal failure. I've said so many times to my players that their futures are what really matter. Whether football is a part of their futures is not as important as getting the education necessary to do something with their lives. Today Fred lives with his family in Phoenix, Arizona, near his brother, Kwamie.

Brooks celebrating a touchdown against Kecoughtan High.

8. Aaron Brooks

The first time I met Aaron, he was a slim tenth grader with a million-dollar smile. Five years later, I trusted him with the key to my house. He would visit me regularly on weekends while home from the University of Virginia. He called me Dad, and we would have our regular mentor-to-man talks. Before long, we weren't worried about college scholarships. He played for the NFL's New Orleans Saints, and I still looked forward to those weekend visits or telephone calls from him.

Some years later, in 1998, I sent a telegram to Aaron at the Peachtree Marriott Hotel in Atlanta, Georgia. He was preparing for his final football game at the University of Virginia in the Carquest Bowl. The telegram said, "Dear Aaron, congratulations on a great season, I will not be able to attend the game. However, this game represents everything you have worked for. Remember, play your best game and have fun, but understand that every time you throw a pass, that pass is worth a million dollars. Good luck, my son—Coach Reamon." Even then, before his pro career, it was amazing how far he'd come since we had first met.

In 1991, Aaron introduced himself to me and informed me that he was a basketball player. I introduced myself as the new football coach at Ferguson High, and I said to him, "Aaron, I have watched you play basketball, but I also saw you play in a football game last season. I agree that you're a better basketball player than you are a football player for now, but I want to show you how to play quarterback as well as you play basketball." He responded, "Okay, Coach," with more enthusiasm than I expected. But like so many kids his age, he remained convinced that basketball was his sport.

My approach as the new coach at Ferguson was to get more players to participate on the football team. I knew that the only way to do this was to establish a relationship with the top athletes in the school, regardless of their sport, and Aaron was just that. I felt that he was the key to establishing credibility with other potential players, because I knew he was well liked by his peers. He was a very intelligent player and had much potential for growth and development. I told him the story of my previous quarterback Fred Lassiter, an All-State quarterback considered to be one of the top players in the country, who was playing at Virginia Tech.

I talked to Aaron about another great All-American high school quarterback named Aaron—Aaron Sparrow of Wilson High School, whose team had won the state championship the previous year. I called Fred and Aaron Sparrow and asked them to talk with Brooks. One week later, on a Monday morning, he came to me and said, "Coach, I met all those quarterbacks you were talking about last week, and had a chance to talk to them. Fred Lassiter said he learned a lot from you and that the exposure he got from playing for you has helped his future." I looked him in the eye and said, "I am glad you met those guys because you can be just as good as they were."

I talked with him about the advantages of being a two-sport player just like his archrival at Bethel High School, Allen Iverson, now of the NBA's Philadelphia 76ers. I had to sell my sport to Aaron, and he had to buy into it. I told him I would show him how to be a great high school quarterback, and then he could choose the sport that he wanted to play in college.

In the summer of 1992, we first went to the Duke University football camp, where the head coach was quarterback guru Steve Spurrier, now head coach of the Washington Redskins. Aaron was being exposed to college coaches, and I observed all the workouts, watching him improve his fundamental skills. Also, if he had an interest in attending the college, this camp experience would help him evaluate the coaches and campus life.

The next week, we went to the East Carolina University football camp; the head coach, Steve Logan, was known by many as an offensive genius. Brooks was very impressive at throwing the ball at an early age, but he picked up a great deal of quarterback technique from the college coaches. During our rides to the camps, we talked of his life and the good behavior he would need to develop. I felt that my ideas were rubbing off on him. He decided to focus on football, and his goal became to be a major college quarterback.

His arm strength and accuracy began to develop in the summer of his junior year. I remember one day at practice, we were doing an offensive team drill called 7-on-7. This passing drill uses a defensive team of only seven players. Brooks' best friend and All-State wide receiver Eric Jones went out on a pass route, and Brooks launched a cannon of a pass to him. As usual, Eric caught the pass with no problem; however, as he walked back to the huddle, he looked down at his right hand. It was bleeding between the ring finger and pinkie fingers. The pass was so hard that it had split the skin between the two fingers, and the deep, ugly little hole frightened him. With Eric's hand split open and Brooks feeling bad for hurting his friend, I felt like I needed to tell them a story to make them feel better. I definitely did not want Aaron to ease up on his passes. I said, "Guys, when I played for the Pittsburgh Steelers, I saw the same thing happen to two Hall-of-Famers, quarterback Terry Bradshaw and receiver Lynn Swann. Bradshaw had such a strong arm, and Lynn was a fluid runner, but had very soft hands. Lynn caught a pass across the middle of the field, came back to the huddle and blood was flowing from his right hand just like yours, Eric. This kind of incident can happen to the best of them." After that, Aaron and I worked not only on his power and accuracy, but on learning to control the release of the ball.

Once the summer practice started, we worked on the drills to improve Aaron as an all-around quarterback. I continue to use and teach others some of the important points I developed for him. I present these points in my quarterback manual and drills. There are five points:

1. Be the hardest worker in the weight room; have a positive attitude at all times.

2. Never give up the fight, because if you quit, your team will quit.
3. Speak to the team on the field with a strong, confident voice, but don't yell. Talk to them and lead.
4. Know your game plan. Always talk game plan with the coach and your teammates. Avoid fault-finding.
5. Take command of the huddle. Get them up to the line of scrimmage. Know the situation and tempo of the game.

All these points deal with life experiences, communication skills, and leadership. I preached these skills to the point that Aaron would become tired of hearing them. However, because he picked up various behaviors immediately, success became easier.

Aaron came from a single-parent home, and they struggled to pay bills and survive. His mother was a very caring but aggressive person. She was big on discipline and just as tough about academics. She was strong-willed with a no-nonsense approach to life, and gave him the best of advice.

They lived in an apartment complex downtown in a low-income neighborhood. It wasn't the worst area, but its residents didn't have much, and it showed. Aaron never complained about what he didn't have, but as he began to be more comfortable with me, he talked about what he wanted. I felt that my ideas were rubbing off on him, and once he decided to focus on football, we talked about his vision to be a major college quarterback and what it would take to earn a scholarship. I preached to him that good grades were the only way to make life better. He had the intelligence; he just needed attention and guidance to be developed into a great student athlete. The reward would be a scholarship to college.

His mother welcomed my relationship with him, and she could tell I had a plan for him. If Mrs. Brooks needed help taking care of Aaron, she was comfortable enough with our relationship to ask me for help. I realized that I opened the door for this type of relationship with her because I deeply cared for his well-being. I would have done more if I could have. I was sensitive to his needs as a young man. One

Christmas holiday break, I asked him if he needed anything. All he wanted was some new clothes, so we went to the shopping mall and I spent over $400. After we bought the clothes, I said, "Brooks, when you become that million-dollar quarterback in the NFL, pay me my money back." He smiled and said, "I will, Coach, and thanks."

His mother did not work at times, but she often spoke of the social services benefits she was receiving, and how these benefits were not enough to pay her bills. She asked me to loan her money to pay the rent. I gave her the money, and I asked her to please pay it back, but she never did. I never mentioned that I didn't really have the money to loan her, I had to borrow it myself. After all the stories I told Brooks about my past, he assumed, like most of his family and friends, that I had a lot of money. He didn't know the truth. I was struggling financially too.

Today, he has never even so much as suggested paying me back, or even asked me to have lunch in order to show some kind of appreciation. But then, I don't ask for anything but "Thank you, Coach," from my players. However, I do tell them, "Friends are made to be used but not to be abused," and it bothers me that Aaron and his mother will not look me in the eye.

During Aaron's junior year in school, we had the opportunity to spend a lot of time together. His mother had temporarily moved out of the school zone, so I would pick him up in the mornings to take him to school. We would talk during the entire ride. We talked about his academics, which were to be the focus going into that year. He was not one to run the streets at night because his mother would not allow that, but the progress reports that his teachers gave me indicated that he was not studying enough. We would have conferences with his teachers, and he would stay after school to make up assignments. He became so involved with basketball at times that he would get behind in studies and I would have to speak to his mother about staying on him.

Tom McGrann was Aaron's guidance counselor at Ferguson High School. He and I worked closely together on monitoring our football scholarship athletes. Since we were both new at our jobs as counselor and coach, the new standards set up by the NCAA would often confuse us. When the NCAA began to implement its Initial Eligibility Clearinghouse Program, these changes caused us some concern for Aaron. He had become a highly recruited prospect in his junior year, and Mr. McGrann had already established a good working relationship him. That was fortunate because Mr. McGrann and I had to work hard to keep Aaron on task and informed of all the eligibility changes. Mr. McGrann would often say, "Aaron has a big smile and is very respectful, but it is difficult to get him to do his schoolwork to get the grades." The smile and personality weren't going to be enough.

Aaron had the academic ability, but getting the reality of the new standards to set in was a definite challenge. At the end of the first semester of his junior year, his NCAA core GPA stood at 2.0. McGrann was able to sit Aaron down and show him where he stood, and what he'd have to do to reach the required 2.5. Needless to say, Aaron got the point and started applying himself. Towards the end of his junior year, the college recruiters started their persistent journeys to Ferguson, and the coaches always pushed for a peek at Aaron's academic record. Mr. McGrann and I worked hard to keep them interested while keeping the potentially damaging news closeted until Aaron's core GPA improved. We figured the GPA was in reach, but the standardized test scores, especially the SATs, were another issue.

Aaron had performed poorly on a pretest (PSAT). He told Mr. McGrann that he had tried, but it was hard. Since he struggled through math and didn't have a good foundation, I decided to pay for professional tutoring before the test. I paid an educator from Virginia Beach $1,200 to tutor him for the test. His mother did not have the money, but because I could relate to his dream of attending a major college, I paid for the tutoring over a three-month period. Once he took the test and made the NCAA requirement, all he needed to do was stay focused on his grades. The tutoring helped his confidence, and he did well enough on the SAT to satisfy the NCAA.

In addition to the GPA and test score issues, there was another problem. Determining which classes would be counted to calculate Aaron's GPA was very complicated with the new Proposition 48H form (Prop 48H), which listed all the classes that the NCAA would use to calculate the core GPA. This form usually was submitted annually, but needed to be updated continually. Mr. McGrann took on the task and found that a couple of Aaron's classes that would have qualified in previous years were no longer on the Prop 48H. Without those classes, Aaron, who by then was considered one of the top quarterback recruits in the country, would not be eligible. Although McGrann had a limited amount of time and no experience, being a true professional, he jumped in and made an immediate and thorough submission to the Clearinghouse. With this done and everything still dependent on the outcome of Aaron's last semester of his senior year and the SAT results, the future status of an eventual NFL starting quarterback remained in doubt.

I was scared that Brooks would not be accepted in the Clearinghouse, and would be my first casualty. If that happened, he would have to attend a junior college—an alternative route. I thought that could be as devastating to Aaron's future as it would be to me personally. Missing two years in a major program as a quarterback would make it more difficult for him to prove how much talent he really had. He would have to start all over again

I managed to get the University of Virginia to offer Aaron a scholarship with the promise from us that we would bring him home on the NCAA requirements. Mr. McGrann worked with Aaron to get all the admissions and financial aid paperwork submitted, and even enrolled him in his fall classes using UVA's telephone registration system. Aaron's final clearance wasn't received until the middle of July. Mr. McGrann and I almost couldn't believe it when we went over his transcript grade for grade, course by course to make sure that he really was eligible. But because of everyone's hard work and Aaron's cooperation he was finally signed, sealed, and delivered!

One of Aaron's finest performances in high school was in a game I called the Shootout at Todd Stadium. The game featured two of the state's best athletes and future professional players: Aaron and his rival, Allen Iverson. We practiced all week on an offensive passing strategy that I felt was critical in order to beat the future state champions, Bethel High School. The strategy was to attack the middle of the opponent's defensive backfield. This task would not be an easy one because of the great athletic ability of Allen Iverson. He played the safety position, which is set in the center of two other backs, and they all defend against the passes. Iverson was the best safety player around. He had quickness, and his recovery range and reaction to a thrown pass near him were exceptional. He was capable of intercepting any pass thrown his way. I have only seen three other players of his caliber in high school football; Ronald Curry of Hampton High School, and David Macklin and Kwamie Lassiter, both of whom played at Menchville High School. David went on to college at Penn State and is now playing defensive back for the NFL's Indianapolis Colts. Of course, we had a great passer in Aaron Brooks, and he would show his talent on that afternoon at Todd Stadium, our home field.

In order for us to be successful, we decided to have three wide receivers run different pass routes with the objective of entertaining Iverson. One of the receivers would act as a decoy by running straight toward him, and the other two receivers would run either a trailing or a crossing pass route. Because he played the safety position, it was Iverson's responsibility to defend against anyone running in the middle of the defensive backfield. Our mission was to force Iverson to vacate that center of the field. He would have to defend against the first receiver coming toward him in his area. It was never our intention to throw the ball to that receiver anyway, especially with Iverson standing there. Aaron threw the ball in the direction of the two other receivers who had been trailing or crossing behind the decoy receiver all afternoon. His passes were as crisp then as they are today.

It turned out to be a great strategy. On one play, our All-State receiver, Eric Jones, ran a crossing pass route behind the decoy receiver, Linwood Debrew. Iverson had to make a decision about which receiver to defend. He stepped backward and turned to defend against Debrew. That allowed Brooks the time he needed, and in a split second, he delivered a bullet pass to Jones, thrown with great accuracy. Brooks impressed us all. Jones caught the ball and raced 45 yards for a touchdown. Aaron completed 15 passes, and threw for 350 plus yards and 3 touchdowns that afternoon.

After months of Aaron's being recruited by East Carolina University, the University of Virginia, and Missouri, he and I went out to a restaurant to eat dinner and review the pros and cons of each school and his decision. I had permission from Aaron and his mother to help in the recruiting process. They realized that I had the experience to communicate with the coaches about problems that could occur. That night, Aaron decided to attend UVA.

Throughout the recruiting process, our main concern became how UVA would utilize Aaron's talent after his first two years there. The strategy was to ensure that he was in the position to be the starting quarterback early enough in his eligibility. Also, we made the UVA coaches aware that we expected a fair evaluation of his talents compared to the quarterbacks already in their program. We discussed and agreed upon a timetable of events. After the conversations among the coaches, Aaron, and myself, Aaron was comfortable with the promises for his future at UVA. As agreed, he would redshirt his freshman year. "Redshirting" is the term for holding an athlete out of competition for a year to save that season of eligibility, when he is still adjusting to the team, for future use. Because college athletes have five years to get in four seasons, the original intent of the rule was to provide a full season for an athlete who was injured early in a year and missed most of the season. It became a way to keep a player from, in effect, wasting a season on the bench when he could be a valuable contributor to the team later. Mutually agreed upon, redshirting is advantageous because every player would prefer a season of eligibility in which he plays a lot over one spent mostly on the bench.

In Aaron's second season I experienced the most difficult time of my private life. In my career there had been many ups and downs. The businesses that I had been involved with, by their very nature, were always filled with uncertainty. However, this crisis involved my family. After six years of marriage, my wife, Brenda, informed me that she wanted a divorce. I had waited until late in life to marry,

Brooks' portrait at UVA.

and the difficulties of married life had presented a new challenge for me. I was unprepared emotionally, and was eventually forced to accept the end of my marriage. But I was determined not to lose custody of my son, Tommy Jr. I had waited a long time to fulfill my dream of being a father, and I had every intention of being in his life on a daily basis.

At that time it was very difficult for a father to obtain custody. It was always assumed that the child would go to the mother. The custody battle that ensued drained me both emotionally and financially, with legal bills from the custody case and the cost of maintaining my home as a single parent. At the same time, I had to prove to the court that I could provide stability for my son as well as day-to-day care. Tommy Jr. was also having a difficult time coping with the breakup of our marriage. So all the time I did not spend working was devoted to him, and this left little time for anything else.

I often wanted to travel to UVA to see Aaron but was unable to do so because of my financial situation and time. Child care was now a major issue in my life. Because my family was very supportive about caring for my son during my work hours, I was reluctant to impose on them by asking for more help on weekends. I was also unable to help Aaron financially as I had done when he was in high school. During Aaron's sophomore year at UVA he asked me for some personal items that he needed for school. It hurt to have to turn him down—I just couldn't afford it—but the worst part was not being able to explain why. I never could reveal my personal problems to Aaron or anyone else in my life. Because I am a loner by nature, sharing my private thoughts and hardships does not come easily. I saw myself as a role model, and at the same time, I saw my divorce as a personal failure. I couldn't explain to him what I didn't understand myself. Perhaps I should have tried, because he must have mistaken my reticence for a rebuff. He must have thought that I had abandoned him. This, however, was far from the case.

Michael Vick had come into my life by this time, and our relationship was just starting to develop. Although Michael and Aaron are cousins, I feel it only natural that Aaron may have developed some jealousy toward our budding relationship. Even though I was very busy with life in Newport News, I still stayed in constant contact with the coaches at UVA concerning Aaron. I tried to fight for him in any way that I could. Nevertheless, as time went on, the tension in our relationship became so evident and awkward that after I talked to Aaron on the day he was drafted by Green Bay, we did not speak again for the next two years.

It wasn't until later, with Michael's NFL draft, that my suspicions about what had gone wrong were confirmed. While I was in New York with Michael, I bumped into Aaron and I asked to speak to him in private. I asked him point-blank, "Aaron, what went wrong between us?" His reply confirmed my worst fears. "Coach," he said in a derisive tone, "I looked after your boy, didn't I?" His reference to Michael was obvious. He had come to Michael's aid during a conflict between agents, helping him out in a sticky situation, the result being that they now had the same agent. I could only look at him and reply with tears in my eyes. "I knew you would, I always knew you would."

Aaron's third year at school was a trying year full of ups and downs. He competed for the starting quarterback spot opposite a fifth-year senior. I had warned Aaron that there might be favoritism among the coaches. I was concerned that his talents would not be utilized to the fullest, and I had been over this with the coaches before Brooks signed for his scholarship. I watched the quarterback evaluation very closely, and sure enough, the other quarterback, Tim Sherman, who was the son of Tom Sherman, an assistant coach on the staff, won the spot. Coach Sherman and I had played against each other in the WFL. He played quarterback with the Charlotte Hornets. Coach Sherman's decision to start his son at quarterback concerned me greatly because I knew that his evaluation of Brooks would be unfair. Objectively, anyone could see that as a parent, Sherman would be biased. I could see the politics at work, and I argued Aaron's case, fearing that Sherman's decision could stagnate his progress.

Coach O`Brien, now the head coach at Boston College, arbitrated the dispute that emerged between Sherman and me. He called me just before the first game, told me both quarterbacks would split playing time. He said, "Coach Welsh told me to tell you that Aaron is much improved and has earned the right to play. He felt like Tim Sherman had a little bit of an edge, but just a bit at this point, so he earned that starting job." I responded, "Coach, Aaron needs to play, and not just a token amount of time." He replied, "Tommy, I will tell Coach Welsh of our conversation," concluding, "Tommy, just note what I am saying about Aaron. We feel he has improved so much; it was a very close competition between the two quarterbacks."

In the first game against Central Michigan, Coach Welsh held true to the promise that Aaron would play. Aaron entered the game midway through the second quarter. On his first play, Aaron rolled out to his left, failed to locate a receiver downfield, and promptly threw an interception on his first attempt. Despite his nervousness, Aaron recovered and showed tremendous poise in the pocket, converting a 13-yard scramble for a first down in the fourth quarter. He had some fun too, running one in from the 3-yard line with a little over a minute left before the half. Maybe he was having too much fun, because Aaron removed his helmet to celebrate before he got to the sideline, incurring a 15-yard penalty. After the game, I talked to Aaron about his performance in my "fatherly voice," as he calls it. I suggested that he watch his emotional reaction after a positive or negative performance on his plays.

I asked him what he thought of his overall performance. He said, "Coach, once I got going, I felt settled and I felt like everything was at a good point, especially when I started to complete passes and make a few plays." I told him that, despite a few minor errors, he looked comfortable out there, and that in college football, it's all about feeling comfortable on the field—it translates into smarter plays and fewer mistakes, especially at the quarterback position. With comfort would come consistency, which is all the coaches are going to expect out of anyone.

Aaron was the backup quarterback that entire season. However, Coach Welsh consistently said, "I want to play Aaron Brooks; that's the way I feel right now. Tim Sherman is the number one quarterback and he is the starter, that's it. Brooks is a great athlete with a great arm, so I want to play him. I think he can help us and that's the way we have been doing it." That help came when quarterback Tim Sherman turned in his worst performance of the season against Georgia Tech, and left the game in the fourth quarter with a sprained thumb.

Aaron grew up as a quarterback that evening, playing against the clock and trying to help pull his team out of a slump and into a victory. Brooks led UVA deep into Georgia Tech territory with minutes left on the clock. He began the drive with a 32-yard scamper to the Tech 27-yard line. He completed a 9-yard pass to wideout Derick Byrd on 2nd and 10, and he tried to hit a wide-open Tiki Barber with a flare pass in the flat. But a Georgia Tech defensive player swatted the ball down, forcing UVA to convert on a fourth and one with one minute to go on the clock. The coaches called a pass play, and Brooks rolled out to the right. Feeling defensive pressure, he threw the ball a bit high, just off receiver Germane Crowell's fingers. The game ended on that play as the Virginia Cavaliers lost with a score of 13-7. As I watched Aaron run that option run play, I said to myself, "Run, Aaron, run!" However, instead of running, he threw an incomplete pass.

Later that night, he called me and we talked about the events of the game. I told him he had played well, but when we talked about that last pass play, I angrily said, "Son, the next time you have a short-yardage situation and are confused about whether to pass or run for a first down, you must trust your legs and think only of making that first down!" He replied. "Yes, Coach." His performance against Georgia Tech was a turning point in showing how much he had improved, and he began to use all his talents and skills to become an effective quarterback. He ended the season seeing his most significant playing time in the season's final two games against Virginia Tech and Miami. In the Carquest Bowl, he ran for one touchdown and passed for another.

In the summer of 1997, we spent a lot of time getting to know the new offensive coach, Sparky Woods. Coach Woods would be the third offensive coordinator and quarterback coach to work with Aaron. The coaching change required Aaron to spend more time in practice sessions and reviewing tapes. However, he was now taking over the reins as the Cavaliers' primary signal-caller. Aaron said he was glad there had been a coaching change—not that he didn't like the old coaches, he just thought his time had arrived and was glad to have a fresh start. He said that Coach Woods taught him to read the entire field on pass plays, and he hadn't done that since high school. He added that with future NFL receiver Germane Crowell and other good receivers returning that season, they knew they would get the ball. Aaron said they would also throw the ball a lot, and the guys would be looking forward to playing and working their butts off.

This level of excitement made communication between us easier. He said, "I feel a tremendous gain between this year and last year as far as my confidence level; I have waited and waited, and now it's my turn." Coach Welsh said, "Brooks has been more decisive, much more in command in the huddle and has much more of an air of confidence about him. Aaron is throwing the ball downfield better than any quarterback since I've been here." He concluded, "I'd like to think we can get a little more out of our passing game this season." I could not help but say to him, "I hope everyone will be patient with him in the early part of the season as he learns and polishes himself as the quarterback in his new offensive system."

Aaron's junior redshirt year started out as a growing experience for him and his teammates and the new coaching staff. I was concerned for Aaron because he was doing well, but not as well as he wanted to. I kept reminding him to be patient. The new offense would mature along with the team, taking a few weeks for him and the system to jell.

Aaron had high expectations at the start of the season. He wanted to prove to people that he was the best quarterback in the ACC. He indicated to me that he was frustrated over some negative media comments. He said, "What they don't realize is that if I had played regularly last season, I would be ready right now at the start of the season. Now I've got to learn this new offense and coaching staff. I'm doing pretty good, but they won't give me no respect." I said, "Aaron, I give you two more weeks and you will set the ACC on fire. You have been improving each game and the team is playing better." The unjust media criticism was too familiar to me as I reflected back to my college football years at Missouri. I begged him to shut his mouth and say no more to the press. In my opinion, he had reached out to them in the wrong way to express his feelings of frustration over things he could not control.

Nevertheless, he went from the outhouse to the penthouse in the eyes of Cavalier football fans. I told him not to voice his opinions about life or racism, or make comparisons with other quarterbacks. For instance, Aaron was inclined to believe that the favoritism displayed over the quarterback was racially motivated. I told him it was irrelevant. I said that mainly because I knew he had to rise above it one way or the other. Such opinions would only get him in trouble with his coaches, teammates, and fans. The media had painted the picture that Aaron rubbed some of his coaches and teammates the wrong way with his attitude and outspokenness. I just kept telling him his break would come.

After a slow start that year, he improved by leaps and bounds. His troubles mirrored the Cavaliers' own problems, but in the fourth quarter of their homecoming game against Wake Forest, Brooks broke through both the Wake Forest defense and the cloud of criticism surrounding his play and rumbled into the end zone for a 25-yard run. That touchdown jump-started the Cavaliers' season and restored Aaron's confidence, helping the Cavaliers go on to win all but two of their remaining games. Subsequently, his performance in the final month of the season was nothing short of remarkable. He was on fire and posting Heisman-like numbers over the final four games. The most important result of the team's success was the self-confidence Brooks gained. He had silenced early-season critics by finishing at the top of the ACC leader board in passing. Brooks ended the season with a passing efficiency rating of 151.0, the seventh-best mark in ACC history. He finished the season against Virginia Tech throwing for 400 passing yards and 4 touchdowns. He had made a statement for himself that day in Charlottesville. He showed that he was indeed one of the best quarterbacks in the country.

During the summer of his final season, he would spend a few weekend nights at my home. Like I said earlier, he had a key to the house. We talked about the upcoming season and his expectations. I told him that this season he should play as if he were playing for the NFL. That's what he wanted more than anything else, except respect. And if he got the respect this year, the NFL would be there to reward him. He called me one evening, happy that *Sporting News* had rated him the seventh-best all-purpose quarterback in the nation, and *Street & Smith's* had given him an All-American honorable mention.

One of the most emotional and memorable games I have ever attended was Aaron's senior-year showcase at Virginia Tech. It was Michael Vick's redshirt freshman year, and Aaron was always pumped up to play Virginia Tech, a great in-state rival. The previous year in Charlottesville, he'd picked apart the Hokies by passing for four touchdowns en route to a 34-20 roasting. This day, he would engineer a 29-point second-half performance, capped off by a 47-yard touchdown strike to former Hampton High School receiver Ahmad Hawkins, which secured the lead for the first time in the game, leaving 2:01 to play. He finished the afternoon with 375 yards of passing, 3 touchdown passes and a 2-point conversion. When asked who I was rooting for to win this game, I said with pride, the first half Virginia Tech and Michael Vick, and the second half the University of Virginia and Aaron Brooks.

Weeks before Brooks' NFL draft, we were talking about pro agents and how to change his workout to prepare for the NFL college players' workout, called the NFL Combines. I said to him that he needed to talk with UVA's then head coach George Welsh and thank him for the experience of playing for him. He balked at the idea, and suddenly he began to cry. I knew what he was feeling, that his heart had been broken. He felt that his talents had not been utilized to the fullest. Watching his tears flow, I reflected on my own lost opportunities at Missouri.

I'd had the same hesitation about talking with the Missouri coaches after my playing days were over, because I too felt they did not utilize my talents. I began to explain to Aaron that thanking his former coach would be helpful. I explained that it takes strong faith in yourself to face a person who you felt did you wrong. I said, "Aaron, be bigger than him because you never know what he will say about you, good or bad." When the professional scouts and other NFL representatives would call coach Welsh for a recommendation of his character and playing ability, Brooks would benefit from positive comments. He took my "preaching," as he calls it, well but reluctantly. I told him that we had to leave the coaches at UVA with at least the perception that there were no hard feelings, and he agreed.

He shared the hurt with me; he felt that other college quarterbacks had gotten more attention and respect then he. I assured him that the best rise to the top. This conversation was hard for me as I mentally revisited the promises made by the UVA coaches during Aaron's recruiting process five years earlier. I remembered the private meetings and telephone calls with the UVA coaches regarding my concerns about not playing politics with Aaron's talents. I could only feel that I hadn't done enough to prevent this pain he was now feeling. After all, this was the whole reason I wanted to coach high school football: to help my players avoid the same pain I felt in college and prepare them for the pitfalls and politics of big-time college football.

Just before the NFL draft, Brooks told me about the day he had met with the Green Bay Packers' offensive coordinator, Mike McCarthy. He was in Charlottesville to check out Brooks, and watched film of the game I had attended against Virginia Tech in 1998. Brooks put on a show in that game by sparking the Cavaliers to a 36-29 victory. Hearing about Brooks' meeting with McCarthy in the film room took me back in my mind to the time before the NFL draft, when I sat down with a Pittsburgh Steelers coach to watch film and talk about my experience at Missouri. I felt this meeting with McCarthy was a blessing for Brooks. Coach McCarthy later said, "The best thing about that visit was getting snowed in. I spent two hours watching film with Aaron, listening to him explain every play and, most importantly, learning more about him." Brooks echoed McCarthy's feeling: "I really got to know him." Brooks said, "Coach McCarthy was the only coach to show a real interest in me. He was the only one to spend time and talk football before the draft." I responded, "I know how you feel. I walked that road before as a player."

I could see the situation coming in the NFL draft; he would be overlooked just like I was. I told him, "That Saturday or Sunday when you get The Call, you're going to be like a little kid and you will know then that you have made it. I know they are going to underestimate you. The system you played in at UVA was not your fault. It was designed to run first, pass second, and the changing of coaches didn't help. However, you are in a great situation. All you want is a chance to prove something. And son, that is all I wanted myself from the professional football business." Aaron said, "You're right, Coach; I'm excited now, but I just can't get my hopes up and then be hurt." I replied, "It's okay to have that feeling too."

The NFL personnel had their doubts about Aaron's future as a signal caller. The questions always arose about him as a prototypical pocket passer. Were his mechanics polished? Was he really a quarterback at all, or merely an athlete? My response to those questions was that Aaron Brooks is all of them and more. He had what they were looking for in an NFL quarterback. He just needed a chance. He needed to continue working on the fundamentals and keep that foundation, and his athleticism would show. "He's a dark horse," Tom Hepler of *Ourlads Draft Guide* said. "What I love is his arm—great arm strength. He throws a darn good spiral and can throw it down the field." Aaron had strong feelings on belonging to the elite group of quarterbacks projected to be drafted before him. He said, "They're all tall and mobile and put up great numbers, but the system helped them out a lot. It gave them a lot of publicity and did them favors. If I had been in one of those systems, I would be a unanimous first-round pick; I believe that with all my heart." I could only respond by saying, "Aaron, I know what you are saying. I said the same words twenty years ago."

Brooks was the ninth quarterback taken in the 1999 NFL draft. That class of quarterbacks taken in the first round included Tim Couch of the Cleveland Browns, Cade McNown of the Chicago Bears, Akili Smith of the Cincinnati Bengals, and Daunte Culpepper of the Minnesota Vikings. Brooks has said many times, and I have echoed his sentiments, that the only difference between him and those quarterbacks was they played four seasons in college and he played two. Of course, we were referring to the political favoritism at the quarterback position at UVA, but Brooks, a strong-willed person, would respond to this challenge too. He said, "Coach, it was sort of cool being on the bottom rung because it's made me keep plugging." Nevertheless, Aaron was an emotional wreck, sometimes buoyant, sometimes scared and anxious.

I have repeated his words to future players because I felt the same way myself before the NFL draft. When the Green Bay Packers traded him to the New Orleans Saints, he was surprised. Coach McCarthy moved on to the Saints as the offensive coordinator, and I was elated for him because of the relationship Aaron had established with him. My first thought when I heard of their reunion was of my own relationship with Jack Pardee years before. Aaron has developed to be one of the best quarterbacks in the NFL—I knew he would be once he was in the right situation, like he has been in New Orleans. Aaron signed a new contract in September 2002 with the New Orleans Saints. The contract is reported to be worth $36 million for six years, with a signing bonus of $5 million. After signing his new contract, he said, "I can now buy myself a new home." What a journey for me in helping to develop him and be a part of such a great story, which all started when I met a kid with a million-dollar smile.

Brooks and another of Coach Reamon's diamonds, Antonio Banks of the Minnesota Vikings.

Michael in action against rival school Heritage High.

9. Michael Vick

On August 9, 1992, Aaron Brooks said, "I got a cousin who's playing for the Boys Club and he's pretty tough, Coach."

"Really, what position does he play?"

"QB, of course! And, Coach," he said, "he's going to be better than me."

"Then he's pretty good, huh, Brooks?"

I stopped by a game and saw thirteen-year-old Michael Vick throw a 40-yard spiral. I decided to keep an eye on him.

The first time Michael appeared at Ferguson High was during the summer weightlifting session and workout before his freshman year. The players were throwing some pass routes. The quarterback position was open since Aaron Brooks had gone off to the University of Virginia. Michael introduced himself to me, and I told him to jump in and throw a few balls. The first ball he threw was so effortless, quick, and strong—I was amazed. I didn't say anything else to him after that, but I knew what to do with him.

We went into the season with a senior veteran team and played the best quarterback at that time, Marcellus "B-2" Harris. Later, B-2 went on to East Carolina University and is now playing receiver for the Calgary Stampede of the Canadian Football League. His father, Reverend Marcellus "Butch" Harris, is a very influential minister and civil rights leader in Newport News. Reverend Harris named his son after himself; and "B-2" is short for Butch the second.

Michael was going to play JV and practice with the varsity as the second quarterback. I watched and handled him very slowly. By the end of summer practice, it was evident that he would be the quarterback of my coaching career. I had seen great NFL passers like Terry

Bradshaw, Joe Gillian, and Joe Montana throw balls, and Vick lacked nothing by comparison, even at his tender age in high school. Because he knew how well I had worked with Aaron Brooks, a relationship between us would be easy to develop.

From the first time I saw him throw a ball, I knew Michael was and would be special. We began to talk a lot during the season at school, and he stated outright that he wanted to be the best, "even better than Aaron Brooks."

He said, "Coach, Aaron told me you helped him get his scholarship, now it's my turn to get mine."

I was glad to hear that, and responded, "Michael, I can make you a star, but it won't be easy. You'll have to trust me."

"Coach, I want to be a star." His sincerity reminded me of myself at his age. Even though I knew exactly how to get him there, putting the strategies together to develop and deliver him would be an exciting challenge.

By the sixth game of his ninth-grade season, Michael had thrown more than 20 touchdowns playing on the junior varsity team. The varsity team had played many of its toughest games, and I moved Marcellus Harris to wide receiver. Doing so would also help him get a football scholarship to college. My philosophy was to specialize players at some point in their careers so that they could earn scholarships.

I decided to bring Michael up from the junior varsity team and to throw him to the wolves against a playoff team, Phoebus High School. I told him to just go out there and do his best and not worry about making mistakes.

We lost the game. He completed just 2 of 11 passes for 30 yards, and was sacked again and again. Nevertheless, I didn't baby him. I just let him know I had confidence in him, and that what others thought was not important. Some of our fans screamed at me for replacing B-2 with a freshman, but the very next week, Michael was 13 for 15, throwing for a single-game district record of 432 yards and 4 touchdowns. And 3 of those touchdowns were to B-2. All of a sudden, he had me looking like a great coach.

My mother had told me when I was young that it was my responsibility, once I had some success, to reach back and bring someone with me. She always reminded me that the reason I was successful was that I had been fortunate enough to benefit from the help of others along the way: teachers, coaches, and friends. I always take this to heart, and saw a great opportunity to put it into practice with Michael. The many talks we had centered on attitude, behavior, and character. I told him a hundred times that I didn't care how intelligent, how driven, or how great an athlete he was, he could not achieve great success without being helped along the way. I gave him what knowledge and life experiences I had, and I expected him to give back, not to me personally, but to the community and other struggling athletes.

In his tenth-grade year, we were preparing for the closing of Ferguson High School. I dubbed 1995 the Ultimate Football Season, and I felt Michael had a great supporting cast. He spent that summer attending college football camps at East Carolina University, the University of Virginia, and Virginia Tech. I wanted to expose him to college coaches and to help improve his skills as a quarterback. The senior players may have been the best overall talent that I have had since becoming a high school coach. On that team were Tramayne Simmons, who later went on to play at North Carolina State University; Marcellus "B-2" Harris, who functioned as a jack-of-all-trades; Dominic Banks, who played at Delaware University; and Damien "Butter" Jones, an all-state defensive lineman. This senior team gave me high hopes, especially with the emergence of Michael Vick at quarterback.

The two most memorable games that year were against Lafayette and Hampton High Schools. In the first game of the season against Lafayette, on the first offensive play, Michael took the snap from center, then turned left and threw a quick, short pass to B-2, who ran for a touchdown to complete a 58-yard play. In the second quarter, Michael took control of the game with some spectacular runs for 58- and 12-yard touchdowns, and passed 7 for 11 for 161 yards and a touchdown pass.

Rough Diamonds

The second game was against Hampton. We had a large group of Ferguson alumni turn out for the final football homecoming. The game turned emotional for the crowd as Vick and B-2 hooked up for a 24-yard touchdown pass on the game's opening series of plays. Then, in the second quarter, Michael's acrobatics on a 26-yard scoring run provided a 14-7 lead, a run that made the season highlights film. Faced with a 3rd-and-20 situation, he scrambled around right end, eluded two tacklers at the 10-yard line and dove over a third into the end zone. We led 14-13 at half time, but a great Hampton team erased the deficit with a big second half to beat us. That Hampton team was led by another great quarterback, Ronald Curry. These two great players would have two more meetings on the football field while in high school but totally different experiences as players in the future.

As with Aaron Brooks, the focus on Michael turned to his performance in the classroom. Sometimes I fussed at him about the most important things in life, and he started disobeying his mother and ignoring his schoolwork. When he brought home a report card with two Cs, two Ds and an F, I made copies of his class schedule and fielded daily progress reports from his teachers.

"I knew I had to make good study decisions on weekends," Vick recalls, "because I knew I had to see Coach Reamon on Mondays." Many weekends during the football season, I didn't have to do much snooping to learn his whereabouts. That's because he often stayed at my house, playing pool and watching football on TV with Tommy Jr. and his teammates. They spent so much time there, I started calling my house "Camp Reamon." In his junior year I helped him get a summer job working at one of the swimming pools operated by Parks and Recreation of the city of Newport News. He was very proud to have his first tax-paying job as a pool attendant.

In 1996, the school division closed the doors of Ferguson High School. The city would build two new high schools and sell the building to Christopher Newport University. In the meantime, the teachers and students had to move to other schools within the city. I was given the option to select the school where I wanted to work, and I chose Heritage High School. Michael was zoned for Warwick; however, because Heritage was a magnet school, he had the option of attending either school. Heritage is located in the southeast part of the city, where I was raised and where Michael lived. There we could continue working together as coach and player. However, the new principal from Heritage did not want me there, and brought in a football coach from the Northern Virginia suburbs.

I was crushed to be turned down for a job in my old neighborhood, where I had contributed so much for so many years and produced the best football team in the city for three straight years. I also felt that since Ferguson was the only school to be closed, I should have first choice of being assigned to one of the new schools, but I ended up being assigned to Warwick High School.

Once the new football coaches were announced at Warwick and Heritage, the Heritage High School principal and football coach went to Michael's home to recruit him to attend their school, and rallied support for their school from his former Little League coaches. His former coaches came to the swimming pool where Michael was working with me and asked him to consider playing at Heritage. They totally disrespected the rules set up by the Virginia High School League on recruitment of student athletes, but Michael told them that his mother had already informed the principal and me that he would be attending Warwick High School.

In the summer of 1996, we stepped up the development of his skills. We attended two summer camps, and I offered private instruction that took him through countless hours of passing and running drills. He threw about a hundred passes a day, and he was introduced to serious weight training. I wanted him to toughen his body so that he could survive a beating. We also worked on scrambling from the pocket, but most importantly, I encouraged the humility that is a hallmark of Vick's game today. I lectured him daily about how a quarterback should comport himself off the field. "You must learn to read, write, and speak well to be a quarterback in America today, and you must know how to communicate with a smile." I held up one of Michael's heroes, Michael Jordan, as an example of this kind of attitude and image of intelligence, personality, and sportsmanship.

Rough Diamonds

A hot topic in the area throughout Michael's high school playing career was the rivalry between him and quarterback Ronald Curry. Michael was overshadowed throughout his high school career by Curry, the nation's top-rated prep prospect in both football and basketball in 1997. I sat Michael down and explained that envy and anger were performance-sapping emotions. I said, "Your day will come." However, Vick so admired the way Curry played that he mimicked some of his moves, and once, when Curry got hurt, Michael sent him a get-well card. But here again, I was blessed to coach a great player who could feel compassion for another great player. Michael and I talked about their competition often, and I would tell him the stories of the rivalry between his cousin Aaron Brooks and Allen Iverson. I always said to him that the difference between him and Curry was the better supporting cast to help make him better, but the key to each of their futures would be who had the adult guidance and foresight to help each make critical decisions.

Michael talked about Curry to writer John Ed Bradley, in an interview with *Sports Illustrated.* "I lived in his shadow," says Vick. "At the end of my senior year I ended up second-team everything. The papers would have a huge picture of Ronald Curry, with poor little Mike Vick down in the corner about the size of a stamp. I never held it against Curry—just the opposite; I was happy for him. But being second was something I had to deal with, and deal with a lot."

The finest high school football game I have ever witnessed occurred between Vick and Curry in their senior year. The stands were filled to capacity, with 10,000 people. Both teams were undefeated with 2-0 records, and people came from everywhere to see two of the best high school quarterbacks in the country. We lost the game after an early lead at half time, but Michael won the heart of every fan. He put on a show as he passed for 300-plus passing yards and accounted for two more scores. His performance was not overshadowed by Curry on that night, though Curry did an excellent job for his team too. Michael said after that game, "I don't mind living in his shadow; I wish I could play games like that all the time and play against great players like Curry every week."

Making that statement convinced me that Michael would one day play on Sundays in the NFL. After his performance in that game, I was even more determined to deliver him to the sports world. I believe that in a different era—before Philadelphia Eagles' Donovan McNabb, Pittsburgh Steelers' Kordell Stewart, and New Orleans' Aaron Brooks—black athletes would have had a tough time distinguishing themselves at quarterback, a position once reserved for Whites. In those days, Michael would likely have become a running back, and sports analysts, forever looking for comparisons, struggle when trying to place Vick in a historical context. They don't know if he better resembles Steve Young with Tony Dorsett's ability or Barry Sanders with Dan Marino's throwing arm. Vick is a new kind of quarterback: elusive, mobile, accurate, and improvisational. He represents the next step in football's evolutionary ladder, an athlete who single-handedly reinvents how his position is played.

I had my hands full trying not to let on that I was convinced Michael would one day be the first black quarterback ever drafted to the NFL as the overall number one pick. I was also afraid that he might let outside forces interfere with his dreams, which, I know in retrospect, had become my dreams too. I preached the expression to him, "If your friends don't have anything in common with you or have the same goals you have, then they aren't your friends." Even though he was not in my home at night, in the light of day I was still determined to help him reach the goals that he had set for himself.

In the spring of his junior year, he was suspended for ten days for bringing a beeper to school, and I didn't lobby to have his punishment reduced. Instead, I helped his parents deliver his class assignments during the suspension, and rigorously enforced the "house arrest" his family imposed on him. He also wanted to play basketball after football season. I did not mind him playing, but his grades were so bad that if he wanted to qualify for a football scholarship to a Division 1 school, they had to improve.

At the end of the first semester, his core GPA was 1.9. To meet the NCAA requirements for a Division 1 school, he had to have a minimum 2.5 core GPA in thirteen classes. He also needed a combined total SAT score of 820. I did not want Michael to have to attend a junior college like I did. I knew that if he would listen, we had the time to turn his academic performance around, but the clock was ticking toward his senior year. I begged him to become a student, and for the first time focus more on academics in school. He respected my opinion and knew I was right.

He accepted the fact that there was no other way to touch his dreams than to improve his grades. I requested a conference with him and his mother, his teachers, and the principal, Mr. Stan Mayo. Everyone was eager to help Michael, but they all agreed that he would have to help himself. His English teacher, Mrs. Jimmie Espich, who has been teaching high school English for twenty-seven years, says, "We all warned him that when he went away to college, there were going to be people hanging around all the time saying, 'Forget about the books Michael, let's go to a party.' We wanted to prepare him ahead of time to deal with those temptations."

We came up with a plan of action for him to improve his core GPA. Our guidance director, Tom McGrann, who had also come to Warwick from Ferguson, printed out an NCAA core course projection sheet for him. This was a computer spreadsheet that Mr. McGrann had developed and used previously with Michael, and his grade point average had improved. Using this tool and getting Michael to commit to a certain performance level, he was able to project an improvement in Michael's core GPA to 2.23 by the end of the semester. We then took a look at the core classes planned for Michael's senior year and printed out the grades it would take to achieve a final core GPA of 2.4. The minimum 2.5 core GPA was a goal to be reached, but if he scored high enough on the SATs, the core GPA could be as low as a 2.2, based on the Clearinghouse sliding scale sheet. A projection sheet was sent to Michael to review and impress upon him what he had to accomplish.

Whether he got the 2.23 or the 2.4 GPA as projected, the objective was simply to raise his core GPA and hope that the SAT scores would be high enough to match his GPA on the sliding scale. Since he was scheduled to take five core classes, he basically needed a B in at least three of them.

Michael wanted to be the best, and Mr. McGrann had been encouraging him to use the same determination and work ethic that he devoted to football, and apply the same respect and obedience to his teachers that he gave me, especially in his academic courses. We encouraged him to believe that if a career-ending injury should come along, developing the ability to put forth his best effort in academics would serve him well in any future endeavors. Not only was this a great motivational tool for Michael, as it is for other athletes, it proved to be the best way to address the academic questions presented by the coaches who were recruiting Michael. Most were extremely impressed and had positive comments about his turnaround. Finally, we set up daily after-school tutoring sessions with teachers and honor students to help him, and we scheduled him for summer school classes.

As with Aaron Brooks, I had arranged for a tutor for him to pass the SAT. He was not eager to work at taking this kind of test. However, he was determined not to let the SAT hinder his chances of getting a football scholarship to college. Again, like Aaron, the tutoring would cost money. I paid $1,800 for his SAT tutoring, and he passed the NCAA's requirements for the test.

After all that help, he and I were very appreciative of his teachers, coming to his rescue. Since that experience with Michael, I have implemented an academic plan of action for my entire football team.

I remember one evening I went to his home to talk with his family about the college football recruiting process. He has always had excellent support from his family, and while they might not have had hands-on involvement with his development, they were a close family and gave great support to whatever he decided. As I walked through the door, I was greeted by at least twelve family members.

They all had come to the house to hear what I had to say, and to offer their own input. We all agreed that the recruiting process would be difficult for Michael. My request to everyone was to let Michael make his own decision, because it would be his four years of college, not ours.

The recruiting process was very easy to manage, and went fairly smoothly. Michael and I decided to choose ten schools that he would be interested in. The selection of the schools was his decision and he could add or subtract a school from the list at any time. Despite our great plan to handle the recruitment process, the turnout of college recruiters overwhelmed us.

The month of May was an evaluation period for the coaches. We had over 100 college coaches visit our school, and the national attention given to both Vick and Curry created a huge amount of excitement. Many recruiters wanted to evaluate Vick. The coaches knew of Curry, but they didn't know much about Vick except that a buzz was spreading around the state. "That Vick just might be the better quarterback of the two," said Kevin Rogers, assistant coach at Syracuse University. The evaluation meant that the college football coaches would assess both his academic qualifications and athletic ability. Therefore, I supplied each of his selected schools with a highlight film of him, an unofficial transcript, and his SAT scores. They also observed him in our after-school study hall and in the weight room, lifting weights. They watched him perform in various agility drills and a throw-and-catch workout with his teammates. After each school's visit, Michael and I would discuss his impression of them. We spoke of the pros and cons of each college program.

One critical issue he considered was what kind of offensive system the school had implemented. The other concern was the quarterback depth chart over a two-year span. The thinking here was that he would redshirt his first year, and the second year he would be able to compete for the starting quarterback position.

This was the same two-year strategy planned for Aaron Brooks in attending the University of Virginia, but I felt the need to warn Michael about the potential politics he could face, as Brooks had.

On a January afternoon in 1998, Vick and I sat down for lunch at Ryan's Steak House in Newport News. Over a hamburger and a heaping plate of fries, Vick finally agreed that Virginia Tech would be better fit for him. In an interview with the *Washington Post,* he told writer Angie Watts that he chose Virginia Tech because it is an in-state school where his mom could easily come watch him play. He said, "I decided that I didn't want to go to Syracuse and live in the shadow of Donovan McNabb. I'm not going to play to live up to the expectations of anyone. I'm just going to do what Michael Vick does best—and that's play football. I want to make a name for myself."

I agreed with his decision to attend Virginia Tech. However, I had one request. If Tech wanted Vick, they had to allow him a redshirt season his first year in college. This meant that he would be on scholarship and be able to practice as well as travel with the team, but he wouldn't play in games. I thought of Michael as a son. So I did what any good father would do to protect his son from getting abused by the system. As a quarterback at a major college, he needed a year to get acclimated to college life, and I was honestly concerned about his academic adjustment.

The months to come would be just as trying as the three years before. My job was not over. His counselor and I felt that we had to deliver him to Virginia Tech in June. In his senior year, he had improved his core GPA in thirteen core courses to a 2.23, but that was not good enough to qualify with the NCAA Initial Eligibility Clearinghouse. We had submitted Michael's transcripts, including the core GPA, the thirteen core courses, and the corresponding SAT score back in late April, and they denied him qualifier status. We could submit a final official transcript after graduation, but Michael could not afford to relax academically. I constantly reminded him how much work it would take for him to qualify, and the minimum grades he needed. He only understood that he had improved in his grades and had a high SAT, but he really needed to understand the difference between a qualifier and a nonqualifier. Qualification would mean he could practice, compete, and receive an athletic scholarship as a freshman, but nonqualification would mean he could not practice or compete during his freshman year.

Michael pushed himself for the rest of the school year. I really admire him, because when things were tough and the pressure was on, he came out swinging. He always listened, and I think that is his greatest asset. But we also had to deal with his worst habit: a tendency to wait until the last minute. When July arrived, he received an approval letter in the mail indicating that he had made qualifier status in the NCAA Clearinghouse.

When I look back on Michael's first year at Virginia Tech, I smile. Without a plan, it would not have materialized. The plan was to have him adjust to both football and academics, and he did both in fine fashion. When he traveled with the team for away games, he would call me the night before the game. We talked about the trip and how his classes were going. From then on, he and I would talk the night before each game, and it turned into a superstition for both of us. We continued this weekly routine until his first professional preseason football game against the Pittsburgh Steelers.

Coach Reamon in the background as Michael announces his decision to attend Virginia Tech.

He brought on great hype by both the media and fans. "I get all this hype and attention, but I haven't even stepped on the field and played a down yet," Vick said. He was perhaps the most highly publicized recruit and redshirt quarterback in Virginia Tech history. However, Head Coach Frank Beamer said enough for both of us about Vick in an article written by sports reporter Angie Watts of the Washington *Post*. "If you haven't seen him play, you're in for a treat; he's really a talented guy. He's got a great release, he can throw the football, he's very athletic, and still the best thing about him is you like being around him.

"He is a good person who will work to be good. I think he'll be a special player for the Big East conference in time, but he's certainly not that guy right now. In our first ballgame, he's going to make some big plays, probably some of them will be for the other team, but I bet he'll be better the next week and even better the next."

Michael's second season was a dream year. The performances and character demonstrated in two games proved to me that I had helped cut and polish a great rough diamond. As I watched the Virginia Tech and West Virginia football game on CBS Sports, I was seeing a child of mine and his team's perfect season begin to tick. Virginia Tech was losing 20-19 with less than 40 seconds left in the game, and its national championship hopes were slipping away. The TV commentators were chastising Michael for failing the biggest test of his short college career: "Got to do something to kill the clock here . . . But don't waste too much time. Michael Vick's wasting too much time right now."

As I watched the upcoming play unfold, I had no worry that Michael would make something big happen. He stepped back four steps, cocked his left arm to throw the ball, then sensed a defensive lineman lurching in from his right. I remember yelling at the TV, "Run, Michael!" He looped in a half-moon path 5 yards backwards, slipping around the defender, and headed down the right sideline. Just past midfield, Vick pulled up short as if he were about to step out of bounds. A West Virginia defender had dived for him, missed, and crumpled to the ground. Michael then sprinted another 12 yards, and skipped out of bounds. It was the play that saved the season, setting up a game-winning field goal as time ran out. I wasn't surprised by his performance, because I have seen him improvise like that before.

At the end of his season I knew a star was born.

Michael's world changed on January 4, in the New Orleans Superdome during a 17-point loss to Florida State in the Sugar Bowl game. In the national championship title game, on national television, Michael, though numbed by defeat, still had accounted for 322 of his team's 503 total yards. With his team trailing 28-14 at the half, he rallied his underdog team to a 29-28 fourth-quarter lead before running out of gas. The final score was 46-29. We talked that night following the game. He was physically worn out, but two Florida State defenders had to go to surgery. He never touched them, but the power of his body jukes was sufficient to buckle their knees. He was honored to have some of the Seminole players line up after the game to pay homage to him as the losing quarterback. A new Michael-mania was born—and it wasn't Michael Jordan.

Two days passed after his dazzling performance in the national championship game. He invited me to join him and his mother at college football's ultimate award show at the Heisman Trophy presentation in New York City. Michael was really shocked to be elected to go to New York. He asked me to help him buy a suit to wear. I told him I would send the money by Western Union. We attended various activities prior to the presentation ceremonies. I was so appreciative to be in the presence of so many former Heisman Trophy recipients. As I sat down and looked around the room, I could not help but marvel at pictures on the Wall of Fame that featured college's best football players of all time. I thought about how I once dreamed to be in this room. However, as I looked over to Michael, realizing that a child of mine was being recognized as one of the best college players in America, I was indeed thankful that he thought enough of me to share this special moment and time.

After the ceremonies, in which he was honored as the third finalist for the Hesiman Trophy, Michael and I took a sightseeing tour of the city and the huge buildings. We walked and talked for hours. I shared with him stories of my many trips to the Big Apple, but none of them was as satisfying to my heart as this one.

Michael said, "Coach, suppose I have a successful season next year like this one. What do you think about me going to the NFL? Some people are saying that I would be a top draft pick if I came out of school early." I responded. "Michael, I agree with those people; however, next year is a long way away. It sounds like you have been listening to people's advice about turning pro. However, son, please don't repeat this subject to anyone else. I think you need to just concentrate on your education and everything else will take care of itself." He said. "Okay, Coach."

The next few months were very busy for Michael. He had to concentrate on his studies and endure overwhelming requests for public appearances.

Some of those appearances were exciting, like his trip to Las Vegas for the ESPY awards. He was honored as the Male College Athlete of the year, and was so excited to be there as the sporting stars converged on him. He met baseball star Mark McGwire, All-Pro football players like Jerry Rice and Payton Manning, and he met his idol, Michael Jordan. He said, "Coach, here I am, a freshman, sitting with those big shots, and the thing that shocked me is that they were all coming up to me."

He was also recognized by his own city of Newport News and its public school system. During the "Michael Vick Weekend" celebration, he was very humble and received numerous city and state accolades.

At the end of the spring months he was drafted by Major League Baseball's Colorado Rockies. Even though he had never played baseball, the Rockies felt he was such a gifted athlete that he would be able to play baseball. To be drafted by a professional baseball team just added to the many other exciting rewards he would receive for an outstanding first year of college football. However, the thought of a baseball career did not last too long. We decided this was not a great idea. On behalf of him and his family, I communicated a thank you to the Colorado Rockies organization and its team representative.

Soon enough, all of the special recognition he was receiving had to come to an end. He had to prepare for spring football. After many more personal chats, we decided to talk with Tech's offensive coordinator, Rickey Bustle, about his plans to utilize Michael's talent as a passer for the upcoming season. We all agreed that he would do a variety of different formations offensively to help Michael improve as a passing quarterback.

Spring and summer continued to be busy for Michael. He traveled to the Playboy Mansion and was recognized as a preseason All-American and made an anti-drug commercial for the NCAA. When he returned after filming the commercial, he called me to say, "Coach, I'm catching up with you now!" I teased him after that commercial, saying, "Just promise me you will play a few more years of college football before going to Hollywood." We both laughed about that.

In early August of 2000, I began to think about Michael some 200 miles away. I visualized the pastoral setting at Virginia Tech, among the sheep and tobacco fields. I could see him rehearsing for another virtuoso performance at Virginia Tech. I also thought it would be the biggest year of his life. I felt this because he had become the nation's most electrifying player, running and passing the Virginia Tech football team to an undefeated regular season and into the national championship game.

That morning, my thoughts flowed, not to his on-the-field exploits but to the mental stability he would need in dealing with the task at hand. I flashed back to my freshman year in junior college. We won the national championship that year, I was the nation's Offensive Player of the Year and All American. I remembered wondering what I could do for an encore in my second year. It was tough, but I made it through all the personal adjustments and media attention that go with that kind of public status. I needed to draw on those memories and experiences to help Michael deal with the coming season.

What he was to experience was far greater than what I had dealt with. The times were very different, yet there were some similarities. The marketing of today's athlete is so much more complex. Football has gone from being just another sport to being mass media entertainment with billions of dollars at stake. We talked constantly throughout the summer of 2000 about the business of football.

There were two areas of concern. The first was how he would handle his new life as a celebrity, and the second was how his quarterback talents would be utilized as a passer in the upcoming season. In fact, the second question had been on our minds since the end of the previous season. We addressed this issue with the coaches during the spring training. They were very receptive and agreeable.

In essence, Michael wanted to throw a greater variety of passes as a quarterback in the offense. Doing so would demonstrate his wide range of throwing abilities, not just his accuracy as a passer or his ability to run plays from different formations, like other quarterbacks in the country who played mundane roles on their teams. Michael thought of the star quarterbacks who played for offenses that used sophisticated formations to improve their passing statistics. Many of these same formations, using three or four wide receivers and relying on a lot of passes, are also widely used throughout the NFL. When a quarterback throws a lot of passes, he gets more media visibility and is credited as a throwing quarterback, and Michael wanted the opportunity to show his skills as a great passer. He was a Heisman Trophy candidate, and the sportswriters' vote is usually for the multipurpose player. If a player is a quarterback, he will be more likely to have outstanding statistics in passing yards and touchdowns. Therefore, for Michael to be looked at as a true major college quarterback, he must show the ability to be an excellent passer in order to be taken seriously by the NFL; and his skills as a passer had to be polished and improved by the time he graduated from Tech. He also wanted to improve on his drop back, pocket type passes to show improved accuracy on shorter passes.

The issue of how his talents would be utilized was more of a concern for me than it was for Michael. Looking back, I don't think he knew completely what was ahead for him. Near the end of the summer break I told him, "Michael it has nothing to do with how many touchdowns you throw. The greater concern will be if you throw two interceptions in the first game; the media will eat you alive." This was the simple truth. The media and the fans would expect more of him because of his performance the previous year. He had been an unknown factor then. Teams would be prepared for him now. Everyone would be wondering if his previous performance was "the real deal." He couldn't just do what he had already done; he would have to do even better.

I said, "Michael, I need you to keep your head straight about everything that's happening around you, especially off the field. I'll worry about your performances when they're good or bad, when you do the right things or the wrong things. The expectations you will put on yourself will be great enough." Later in the season, Michael would say in an interview with writer Richard Rosenblatt of the *Commercial Appeal* of Memphis, Tennessee, talking about our discussions of the coming season, "It was like Coach Reamon saw all of this coming. It was like he looked into the future and just knew." I sit back now and marvel at that statement. Michael's life changed in dramatic fashion, but he was ready. And took nearly everything in stride. Some things were tough, like going out to eat in Blacksburg with friends—he was besieged by fans.

At Tech's annual Fan Day festivities that summer, there were two lines for autographs: one for Michael and one for the rest of the team players. His line nearly doubled the length of that of his teammates, stretching nearly the length of a football field. Because Michael is a team player, this bothered him. In conversations I had with Coach Beamer, he said, "Vick is clearly uncomfortable with that aspect of his fame. We're doing our best to make him feel as normal as possible." Even though Coach Beamer had a vested interest in a happy and contented Michael, he constantly said, "Michael Vick's refreshing. He hasn't changed. He's still a team guy. He likes to compete. And the more that is at stake, the better he is. He needs to continue to develop. There is more for him to learn at the college level."

Coach Beamer's assessment was right about Michael's need to continue learning. We knew that his performance and recognition in his freshman year were due also to a great supporting cast of talented teammates. This season would be different. Several of those players were gone. Most of the attention would be on him alone. The first four games of his sophomore season, the offense ran the ball. A new star at Tech was born in running back Lee Suggs. I would say the first month of the season the offense lived on the ground, not in the air. Michael played great and showed many of his talents as a great athlete in every game, but he was frustrated by being asked to do so much offensively, and the risk of injury was increasing.

The young offensive line needed time to grow and mature, but Michael didn't have time. He appeared to be running for his life, not to be sacked on many of his pass plays. For most quarterbacks trying to woo the Heisman trophy voters, an abysmal 5 of 7 pass completions for 61 passing yards would be a campaign killer. In the game against Boston College, Michael's normally reliable throwing arm had trouble hitting the "broad side of a barn." He then resorted to using his feet to kick Boston College's tail. He ran wild on artificial turf for an amazing 210 yards rushing and a dazzling 82-yard touchdown. It's funny that Sunday night after the game he said, "Coach, I wasn't too disappointed in my performance because the fans there made me feel great. They were chanting from the stands, 'We want you [Vick] to be a Patriot next year, we want you to be a Patriot.' I had to laugh, Coach, because it wasn't until after the game that I realized that they do have an NFL team there." I responded. "Michael you did great, keep it up and don't worry about those things you can't control."

But soon, he was getting tired of all the talk. The West Virginia game was important to him because of the previous year's game and his last-minute heroics that helped send his team to the national championship game. He said, "To heck with all the hype. I'm ready to let it all loose and just play football. I'm tired of trying to impress everyone on the outside, most notably those with a Heisman Trophy vote." He wanted to prove himself against West Virginia on ESPN for a national audience. He wanted to have a great game performance in pass statistics. I knew he was pressing himself. He was trying to do too much. The Tech offense was not well balanced with run and pass plays—the running game was carrying them. When they wanted to throw the ball, it was the same old story as in the previous weeks. Michael Vick would drop back to pass, the offensive line's blocking would break down, and he would take off running. He was frustrated. The week before the Syracuse game, an article written by Boston *Globe* columnist Will McDonough came out saying, "The word is that Vick is going to leave Virginia Tech and go into the NFL draft next year."

That article began rumors throughout the Tech community for weeks, and they would not stop. It did not help him to have these rumors flying around while he was trying to improve each week playing against the teams he had to face. In a 37-34 win at Pittsburgh, late in the first half, he injured his right ankle. This high ankle sprain would keep him from full speed for rest of the season. The preparation for the conference showdown game in Miami would further frustrate him, and I felt helpless and unable to ease his pain. To play in that Miami game, he needed a miracle to recover from the injured ankle. Each night that week before the trip to Miami, he would give me an update on his progress. He was walking around with a slow limp, his sprained ankle encased in a protective boot. He sat out of practice most of the week. I asked, "How do you feel?" He answered. "I'm better, but I'm still not able to do what I know I can do."

The day of the game, he called me to ask my opinion of an injection of cortisone in his ankle. I said. "No, absolutely not." I told him of my experience in pro football with injections when I ended up in the hospital. "No injections of any kind," I reiterated. I said, "If it was done during the week to help your ankle heal faster, then I would support that type of therapy. But not on a game day." I left the telephone thinking that he would not play much, if any. As I watched him enter the game in the first half, my heart was full of pain, for I knew he was hurt and disappointed. Within the first series of offensive plays he executed, he attempted to run an option play. I exploded with anger. He was then sacked twice. I was furious. I called his mother, who was watching the game at home, and voiced my disappointment in the coach's play selection. I felt that they had shown little regard for his physical well-being by putting him in that situation. Miami beat Tech that day and then went on to win the national championship. However, as for Vick's relationship with Tech, for the first time I began thinking of his future in the NFL, before a career-damaging or -ending injury might occur.

Michael played hard to finish his second and, it turned out, final collegiate football season. He said, "Coach, I understand what it's all about now. Two years ago, people were just learning my name. I could walk on campus and not many people would bother me. I was just another quarterback with big ambitions. But thanks to you, Coach, and others, I had a master plan. I thought I would go to college, and learn during my first season; the second season I would get better, and the third and fourth seasons my career would take off. Now things have happened real fast, a little quicker than I dreamed of. Everything is totally different. In just two short years I have become a money-making product for Virginia Tech."

What today's major college programs thrive on are super athletes to help them win games. The Virginia Tech coaches and community were experiencing what Florida State, Miami, and many big-time programs go through. They want to win games and make big money to build big buildings and have stadium expansions to make more money. Michael was seeing this. For the first time he now understood what I had always said to him about major college football. He said to me, "Coach, major college football is just about big business."

On December 15, 2000, Michael called me about 11 A.M., to tell me that a pre-Gator Bowl press conference was scheduled and he wanted to know what to say to reporters. I told him to say that he would be returning to Virginia Tech and make no comment from that point on. He later called and told me those words about staying at Tech worked with the press. I suggested that he not say any more to anyone. He wanted me to set up meetings with Lee Steinberg, known as the guru of quarterback agents, who had represented the most college underclassmen who went on be the top NFL draft picks. The other agency was Michael Jordan's agency, SFX, with top agent David Faulk, whose marketing skill is known throughout the country.

On the meeting night at my house, they called and introduced themselves to him. Each was very professional and general in conversation. Their professionalism was the main thing I wanted Michael to see and hear. After that, he went back to school for the Gator Bowl practice, but he would come back to Newport News for a few days prior to leaving for the Gator Bowl game. The very last thing I said to Michael before he boarded the plane for Jacksonville, Florida, to play against Clemson University was, "Michael do not discuss any future plans. Just say 'no comment' to the press."

First thing the next morning, the phone rang, and it was Frank Beamer, the head coach at Virginia Tech. He told me that Michael was talking too much to the press and the questions and answers presented to him created too much controversy. The key words Michael had added were that he was "thinking it over" since his last press conference at Tech. I called Michael to say, "Son, do not say any more. Have a great game and we will talk when you get home."

On the day of the game, Michael put on an extraordinary performance over Clemson. After the game, on the field with a TV camera crew following him, the reporter asked him about his plans to stay or go professional. He said, "I want to go home and talk to my mother and Coach Reamon." Although it was personally gratifying that he said that on national TV, the telephone calls began to pour in at my house. The next few days I averaged ten messages a day from reporters and new sports agents. I did not return the calls.

When Michael called me from the airport after leaving the Bowl game, he asked me what I thought he should do. I said, "Michael I will not tell you what to do; you must make your own mind up. The one thing I want to do is protect you from making a decision before listening to professional people that can give you sound information." At the end of our conversation, he said that Coach Beamer was coming to town on Thursday to talk with me. I thought to myself, maybe Michael really knows what he wants to do. If he does, then a public announcement to everyone must be presented correctly and maturely. His decision must be seen as positive and be carefully thought through.

Michael soon asked me to set up the meeting with the agents. Prior to him telling me this, I was unaware of how seriously he was thinking about leaving Tech. I assumed he was totally confused, just as he had been when making up his decision on what college to choose when coming out of high school, but this decision was much bigger and the ramifications were huge for a lot of people. My only hope of helping him make the right decision was to make sure he listened to both sides and got all the information he needed. After the Gator Bowl, Michael and I talked and agreed to have a meeting with Coach Beamer and staff regarding why he should stay. We would also have an informational meeting with three or four agents to get the pros and cons of the decision to come out. We would consider then how they would guide him toward preparation for such a decision. I asked Michael and his mother, Brenda Boddie, if they wanted any other people to attend the meetings.

Mrs. Boddie said, "Yes, my sister will be attending." Nothing was mentioned about Michael's father attending. At the time, I saw nothing unusual in this, but later it became important to me because Michael's father, Mr. Michael Boddie, accused me in a *USA Today* article prior to the NFL draft of not inviting him to this meeting. To be honest, he had never attended a meeting with Michael and his mother that I had been a part of since I met Michael Vick in the ninth grade. However, I could see a very caring man in Mr. Boddie.

The meetings on Thursday started at a Virginia Tech alumni business building. The facility was first-class, including a telephone conference system on which Michael could talk to other people he thought could give him sound advice. Coach Beamer and three assistant coaches and an NCAA compliance person attended. They put on a classy presentation that explained issues of education, maturity, a solid injury insurance policy, the promise (or possibility) of being the 2002 top NFL draft pick by Houston.

The Houston Texans' general manager, Mr. Charlie Casserly, presented good sound suggestions why Michael should stay in school for one more year. He was speaking on this issue with the assumption that the Texans would draft Michael as the NFL number one pick in 2002. He had a speakerphone conversation with the general manager of the Indianapolis Colts, Mr. Butler, Colts quarterback Payton Manning, and Philadelphia Eagles quarterback Donovan McNabb. All these individuals took time to talk of their experiences and the pros and cons of staying in school for one more year. Michael and his mother were impressed, but appeared overwhelmed with all of the information. The conversations were very respectful, but the Virginia Tech staff felt that Michael was listening to agents out there who did not have his best interests in mind. As I watched and participated in a few questions on Michael's behalf, I could see and feel desperation in the eyes and voices of the coaches who were trying to hold on to the athlete who had taken their program to the highest level of college football, and given it the respect and money that comes with it. I refused to comment to anyone on my personal thoughts, because my role was to help Michael gather information.

The meeting ended with the coaches showing some of the Gator Bowl on a huge TV screen in one of the rooms there. At that time, the coaches were unaware that Michael would meet with agents that afternoon. That afternoon at the law office of a friend, Michael, his mother, and aunt drove up. I met them at the car and informed them that the agent Lee Steinberg had brought some of his clients to meet him in a limousine. I didn't tell him who they were until he got in the office. Michael and his mother were shocked but enthusiastic to meet All-Pro quarterback Warren Moon and Virginia Tech alumnus Bruce Smith with Lee Steinberg. I said to Lee, "You know how to make an impression."

Michael really appreciated the gathering of these people to talk with him, and said so graciously. The players did all the talking to him about making a decision to go pro. They never encouraged him to come out of school. They warned about potential injury, and agents who surround you and manipulate you with money and girls, and other pitfalls. Michael said to me after the meeting, "Coach, I didn't know all this was so important. I just wanted to make a decision to go play pro football." I said, "There are a lot of things that go into your making this decision, and how you do it will only help your perception in the public eye."

By the end of the meeting I had received another phone call from the SFX agency's top man, David Faulk, that he would be late flying in from Florida. I told Michael this was a good time to go get some rest and something to eat. I was mentally exhausted, so I knew he was overwhelmed. I decided to run to my house to check on Tommy Jr. and my babysitter. When I stepped through the door, Tommy Jr. came up to me and said, "Daddy, the six o'clock news reported that Michael was meeting with pro agents." I was alarmed that this was being announced. Who could have told anyone that a meeting was going on? We figured the agents leaked this information.

The next meeting with the SFX agency was very impressive, but Michael was dead tired. You could see it in his face. He was unaware how good these people were at what they do. They put on a film presentation about "Michael Vick's Future." The agents respected my request to just tell Michael the benefits of having agency representation if and when he made a decision to come out of school. They never mentioned specifics, and they gave him objective and unbiased advice about making a decision to come out of school as an underclassman. Even though they are known for their marketing of great athletes, at no time did they tell Michael to leave school. At the end of the meeting, I stated that if Michael made a decision to come out of college, he might request to meet with them again to discuss and seek agent representation, and I thanked them for their information. Michael could feel good that even though the decision would be tough, at least he had more information to help him make it.

After the meeting, I told Michael that he should feel good about his situation and that he should take the weekend off and decide what he wanted to do. By the time I got home, I had twenty-one messages on my telephone. Three of them were from Frank Beamer at Tech. It was too late to call any of them back, and I didn't. All of these calls made me wonder what my role in Michael's life was at this point. I viewed myself as his friend, and for years I had stressed the importance of presenting a positive image. I didn't want him just to be a talented athlete. I was every bit as interested in the kind of man he would grow into off the field. He delivered on the field with great performances, which is critical, but the perception the public had of him as a person off the field was just as important. Now it was essential for him to watch what he said and get good advice.

I began to think that if Michael asked me for advice, I would have to give it. I thought of Michael as a son, and as his father I wanted him to get his degree from college. The teacher in me also wanted the same. However, as a former player and coach, I viewed Michael as a hot product in a big business. For many years I have told my players, Michael included, that playing in a major college football program is a business and they are products. I say to them that their scholarship is payment for their college education; therefore, they must get that degree. If they are fortunate enough to go to the ultimate level and play professional football, then they are the lucky ones.

On the other hand, Michael's trade was football. He dreamed of being in the situation to play professional football, the younger the age, the better. He didn't want to be a doctor, lawyer, or teacher. It was once necessary for athletes like myself to think of their lives beyond their playing days, and be prepared with a "real-world" skill to fall back on. But in today's game, the top athletes can make enough money to live on for the rest of their lives, and Michael had that level of ability.

The possibility that Michael could be injured if he returned to play one more year at Virginia Tech was also a critical concern. The timing of his success, and his visibility in the national sports media had made his name very marketable. This timing might not ever occur again. He had to respond. Now.

He had a chance to make millions of dollars. I felt that if he turned professional then, even though he would not be getting his degree, he would at least be using the trade learned in college to make his life better. Because I was not Michael, I was not going to tell him what to do. I did, however, share my opinions with him.

On Sunday, Michael's mother called me to say that Michael was very upset with her and his aunt because they had been discussing his situation. She went on to say that he was not being honest with me regarding talking with agents. However, whenever they tried to talk to him about his decision in general, he became upset and left the room.

After listening to what she had to say, I could only respond by saying that Michael was open to see whomever he wanted to. She said, "He just gets upset with me." I promised her that I would talk to him.

I called Michael and asked him to come by the house. When he arrived, we talked first about the previous day's events, and gradually our conversation turned into a discussion on his future. Then he revealed to me that he had decided he wanted to come out of college and go pro.

I tried to tell him to be businesslike about the decision and to get away from this for the weekend. I said, "Congratulations; you should feel proud and relieved. But your mother spoke about some discussions with an agent that you were upset about." He then revealed to me that he had met an agent in Jacksonville, Florida, during the Gator Bowl game week. Then he asked me what I thought of a black agent and I said, "Michael just like when you were recruited out of high school to college, the comfort level you feel with the people you meet is what makes a good business relationship work." I continued, "Whoever you want as an agent is okay with me." He asked that I meet with them, and I said, "Sure, if you want me to."

I strongly stated that he must handle the Virginia Tech situation very carefully and professionally. I advised him to show maturity in his decision—he should hold a press conference and invite Coach Beamer. The deadline for the NFL draft declaring was the following Friday; he had a lot to do. He also had to return to Virginia Tech to get his transcript to send to the NFL office along with other papers. I volunteered to begin those jobs the following morning if he wanted me to, and I said adamantly, "Michael, you have to talk to Coach Beamer immediately."

My role in his decision was not important, but how Michael presented himself to the public was. The reality of his relationship with Virginia Tech and the public perception of it was my concern. I told Michael that he did not want to be insensitive toward the educational aspect of the decision and how others would see it. Kids saw him as a role model. I told him, "The public must understand that you care about the experience of being a student athlete in college, even though you've decided on a different route for your life." Also, I reiterated my concern that he communicate with Coach Beamer and get his blessing. We wanted positive things said about Coach Beamer, and to have him see this as a mature, positive step for Michael.

After our conversation, I talked to Beamer every day for three straight days. He was concerned, but polite. I let him know I appreciated how difficult it must be for a person facing a very important career issue. The possibility of losing the star player who had helped take his program to the top level of football programs in the country was upsetting for him, naturally, but his comments were calm and precise regarding Michael's maturity and the need for him to play another year in school. I told him that I personally appreciated his coaching and handling of Michael's college football career, and that Michael's decision had been difficult. However, I asked for his public support of Michael's decision. I also said that if a press conference were scheduled for Michael, I hoped he would attend. He agreed to do so.

We discussed the option of Michael staying in school once more during the conversation, and he proposed an insurance policy to protect Michael against a career-ending injury, which was his best selling point. I suggested he call Michael, and he said he would. I did not indicate to Beamer that any public comments about an insurance policy might make him look desperate. He said, "Tommy, I will have no more to say, then." I felt that Michael's decision must have Beamer's blessing, regardless of how disappointed he would feel by losing him to the NFL.

The next day, Michael said he had told Coach Beamer and Rickey Bustle of his decision to turn pro. I suggested to Michael that a press conference be set up at a central site. It could not be at Virginia Tech because the coaching staff was out of town, and it could not be at Warwick High School because many people felt that Michael's leaving school would send out the wrong message to students. I suggested having it at our local Hampton Roads Boys and Girls Club, where he had spent a lot of time as a youngster. He agreed. The press conference was set for Thursday, and the NFL Draft declaration day was that Friday.

I was concerned about the many details of setting up this public announcement in which Michael would declare himself in time for the NFL draft deadline. I told Michael he had to complete various papers and forms requested by the NFL, and reminded him that he had to travel to Virginia Tech to get a copy of his transcript to submit with these papers. I told him I would call him that next morning to finalize the details. I never heard from him. At about 11 A.M., I got a call from Virginia Tech that Michael was on campus with an unidentified man picking up his transcript. I was confused. I was now concerned that Michael was trying to tell me he no longer needed my advice. I had so many thoughts.

I called his mother, and she said, "Coach, Michael needs to talk with you about these agents." I responded, "Mrs. Boddie, if Michael has an agent he likes who can do what is necessary and needed, I'm happy for him." I got off the telephone. My immediate thought was that Michael was afraid to tell me he had selected a different agent from the ones he had requested to meet before the Gator Bowl, afraid that I would not agree with his selection.

Later that night Michael called me. He said. "Coach I know you are wondering what is going on. I have an agency that I like and want them to represent me, but I want you to meet them." I responded, "Michael if you're satisfied with these guys, then I will be too. But, Son, we have talked about this serious issue of agents for almost a year now."

He said, "Coach, I understand, but I need you to meet them." I went to his home. I did not want Michael to think I was disappointed in him because of the way he had selected an agent. He had not informed me he was talking to any other agents, and I was concerned about whom he had gotten involved with and how. It was not important now. What was important was that the public supported him in his decision.

Many times over the years I had said to him that perception is critical. There are so many talented athletes today, teams can pick and choose the personalities they want to have in their organization. A player who is seen as difficult or dishonest might have a hard time succeeding in the NFL, no matter how great his talent. It wasn't only Michael's playing ability that had captured the media's attention, it was his charm and refreshing openness. Would his decision change the public perception of him?

On the drive over to Michael's house I thought about our relationship. We had spent many hours discussing his dreams. What bothered me terribly at first was that he had not trusted me or had enough faith in our relationship to tell me of his discussions with another agency before now.

So I was disappointed, but as with all of our children, we want the best for them, even when we do not agree with some of their actions and decisions. Thus I was determined to give Michael my full support. I wanted what was best for him and his family. He apparently had pressures within himself that I didn't know of and he felt he couldn't share with me. Regardless of his actions on that one occasion, Michael has always been more than a student or a player to me, and he still is.

The press conference was a success because Michael presented himself in a very mature way. Coach Beamer did attend, and gave Michael his blessing, even though I could see his eyes were full of tears. This was a heartbreaking experience for him and the Virginia Tech football program, but Beamer demonstrated what a class act he is the way he handled Michael's departure from Tech to the NFL.

After the press conference, Michael and his agents prepared for the NFL draft day, and he and I did not talk for months leading up to it. He appeared to have made a mistake with the hiring of the first agents. However, in a very businesslike way, Michael corrected that mistake with the help of his cousin Aaron Brooks. It was very fitting that Aaron would come to his rescue, because in high school it was Aaron who first had come to me and said, "Coach I have a cousin I would like you to take care of." So now, not too many years later, Aaron would tell his agent, Andrae Colona, to take care of his cousin.

Michael invited me to attend the 2000 NFL draft. I drove to New York City with Tommy Jr., and my mother and stepfather. As I sat there in Madison Square Garden watching the activities, I was so happy for Michael, whom I had come to love as a son. As predicted by everyone, he was chosen as the number one player in the NFL draft by the Atlanta Falcons. After his selection, we headed home, and Michael headed to Atlanta, his new home. I did not talk to Michael for months after the draft. One day, he called me to invite me to Greenville, South Carolina, to observe him in his first preseason practice as a rookie. Marcus, his younger brother, also an All-American high school quarterback (and one of my most recent diamonds), traveled with me.

The Atlanta Falcons coaches let me sit in on a couple of quarterback meetings. I was so grateful to them to let me observe those meetings. As I sat there and listened to the offensive play terminology, I leaned over and whispered over to Michael, "I am glad you had that experience of redshirting at Tech."

"Thanks to you, I know how to handle not playing immediately. I will be patient and learn all of this new terminology and then play for ten years," he whispered back.

"Michael, I know you'll do exactly what you say."

That meeting was the last time I spoke to Michael in person. I left him, saying, "Michael, it's time for me to let you go." Little did I know that doing so would be even harder than I had imagined; but like any parent, I had to let my son find his own way. Finally, I said, "Please don't change that humbleness you so wonderfully project to people, and enjoy your life."

In the 2002 football season, Michael was the starting quarterback for the Alanta Falcons. He made the immediate impression to the NFL world that the best was yet to come.

On the day he announces his decision to attend Virginia Tech, Marcus looks on as big brother Michael says a word or two for the press.

10. The Chain of Diamonds Continues

Marcus Vick

Marcus is a very quiet, sensitive, aggressive, and impressionable person. I watched him as a football player for the first time in his freshman year. While his brother Michael was a redshirt freshman at Virginia Tech, Marcus was throwing a football at junior varsity practice. Everyone asked me the same question, "Is he going to be a quarterback like Michael?" I wondered about that too, and the first time I saw him throw a football, it was obvious that his mechanics and form needed a lot of work. I remember asking Marcus what position he wanted to play. When he said he thought he would like to play running back or receiver, I did not respond immediately. Instead, I went to my assistant coach, Curtis West, whom I had coached as a quarterback. I always look for a quarterback who is talented enough to play running back like I once did and is athletic enough to play receiver. He fit my notion of a young, raw talent to begin the developing stages in my program for the quarterback position. Marcus was blessed to have the same savvy and aggressiveness as his brother Michael. I told Coach West to try training Marcus at quarterback, work on his mechanics, and see what happened.

I soon saw improvement in his quarterback skills. Later in the junior varsity season, I told him that when his time came, I would help to make him a great quarterback, but I did not put pressure on him to play quarterback in his first two years of high school. He understood my philosophy that a player must wait his turn. The quarterback slated to play at that time, Dontrell Leonard, is presently the starting quarterback at Norfolk State University. The competition between the two was fair, and as I have said so many times, the players who buy into what my program represents and do what is asked of them will be competitive when it counts most. Dontrell was a senior and wanted to go to college, and his parents had the same dreams. He deserved to have the opportunity to make something out of himself and get a college scholarship.

In Marcus' tenth-grade year I sent him to Hampton University Football Camp. I told him to split time working as a quarterback and receiver. I said, "Marcus, I need you to understand that I don't care if you think that you may be a better quarterback than Dontrell. He came to this program to get a scholarship. His parents want that for him too. I need you to play another position this year. Next season will be your turn, and I will do everything possible to make you the best quarterback in the country." He agreed, and the subject never came up again. This showed me his loyalty to my system.

He accepted his role as a receiver and displayed extraordinary talent. By the seventh game of the season, Dontrell Leonard had received four college football offers for a scholarship. I was excited for Dontrell because he had played well. However, it was now time to introduce Marcus as a quarterback.

Marcus and I talked about the things we had to do to get him ready for the next two years. Attention to academics needed to be his primary focus. He had been there for the struggle with his brother Michael. I visited with his parents, and told them that after going through this issue with Michael, I did not want to have to fight with Marcus. Marcus and I started spending more time together. We traveled to football camps and developed a different kind of relationship than I had had with Michael. Marcus was very quiet, and and trying to get him to talk about anything was like pulling teeth out of his mouth. So it's easy to see how one weekend visit he made to my house stands out in my mind. I had to cut the grass in my yard, and he spoke up to say, "Coach let me cut the grass for you, I have never cut a yard of grass before. This would be my first experience because I have lived in an apartment all my life." When someone hardly ever speaks, then finally opens his mouth to ask for something, how can you say no?

The summer of his junior year was not only important for him but was a big year for his brother as well. They both would be starting quarterbacks for their respective teams in the upcoming football season. Marcus Vick was introduced to the high school football world at the first game of the season with Oscar Smith High School.

"I was hoping he wasn't as good as his brother," said Bill Lyons, the head coach of Oscar Smith and former Warwick High School football coach. That comparison to his brother would become of great importance to Marcus's success. I say this is because on that same Saturday in Blacksburg at Virginia Tech stadium, his brother Michael was introducing himself to the country with an outstanding performance against James Madison University.

I was very careful when comparing the two brothers. In teaching Marcus quarterback skills and football strategies, I always referred to quarterbacks other than Michael. I did this in an effort to keep Marcus from thinking of how his brother did this or did that. I knew that with the success I'd had with Aaron, Michael, and Dontrell, I had his undivided attention for learning what he needed to learn.

His first year was great. He was the top quarterback in the area by far. He was learning and improving with each game. The game that I will always remember was his 300-plus passing yards performance against the district powerhouse Hampton High School. Unlike Michael and Aaron, he was not being challenged as the best player in the area. Instead, he was being compared to his brother. In private talks, he always shared with me how excited he was to compete and follow in his brother's footsteps. I always admired that about him. He was very comfortable about his feelings on that issue. Later, when his life started changing due to Michael's success, he could not hide some of his frustration. He was being exposed to the media marketing his name, and celebrity status was knocking on the door. My role, as always, was as a sounding board to his private thoughts about the attention he and his family were receiving. I kept saying to him, "Marcus, this is your time and your show." By the end of his junior season he had thrown for 2,180 passing yards and 22 touchdowns, rushed for 700 yards and 10 touchdowns. The stage was set. He said, "Coach, I can't believe the season I have had! It's great!" I replied, "Marcus, we just got started."

Academics and SAT scores became a concern in the spring of his junior year. I paid for the SAT tutoring, just like I had done for Michael and Aaron. This was all going on while Michael was preparing for the NFL draft and I was setting up the press conference.

I was proud of Marcus' commitment to focus on the test preparation, all while the media attention on Michael and the NFL caused a major change in his family's lifestyle. Yet, Marcus knew what he wanted for himself. I sometimes thought that the family left his academic and athletic career to me, and at times I felt I was being used by them. But their child's well-being was more important to me than anything else, and Marcus himself was extremely committed to doing what was necessary to succeed.

I told Marcus that I would market him to be as big as the media wanted him to be, but he must do his part. He had to get his grades straight and do the right things. I was very good at selling him to the public, but to do this, I made certain public statements comparing his talents to Aaron's and Michael's. I talked with each of them, to remind them not to take it personally. Athletes are often jealous, and worried about feeling second-best. However, they both knew my comments about Marcus' talents compared with theirs were only to benefit his standing in the media.

Attention on Marcus heated up after an *ESPN Magazine* article about the excitement surrounding Michael's entry into his first NFL training camp with the Atlanta Falcons. The media and college coaches were calling me, asking for comparisons of the two brothers and their cousin Aaron Brooks. Again, I publicly gave the media what they wanted to hear. I told them he was better than Michael or Aaron, going into his senior year in high school. I told Marcus that I would promote him and that he had to be prepared for the attention. He was also exposed to his brother's influence. I convinced him that this was his time, not his brother's or cousin's.

Marcus has that inner strength, along with a strong desire to be the best. Yes, people could say that he was getting attention because of his brother. I would reply, "So what?" It shouldn't matter to him why he was being compared to his brother or whether he really was better.

What mattered was that he was getting the attention he needed to be in the position to help his future. He would have options to be recruited by the best colleges and enjoy the recruiting process for himself. I was Marcus' coach, but I became a fan of his because of his work ethic, both on and off the field. He worked on every aspect of his character as a person to be prepared to take on the national attention he was receiving, regardless of the reason.

I believed that he would improve as a quarterback by the end of the summer camps tour I had set up for him. The *ESPN Magazine* writer traveled with us to various summer camps prior to his senior season.

A few weeks after the tour, Marcus and I went to Greenville, South Carolina, to see Michael in his first Falcons training camp. I said, "Marcus, the public likes stories like yours: a successful brother and the younger brother following in his footsteps. However, knowing that, the press can make you look great, but they can tear you down just as easily." So the objective was to present him to the public in a positive way on and off the field.

On the field, Marcus was definitely his own man. He thrived on tough game situations, and he did the same in the classroom. He completed a great senior season with 2,012 passing yards and 18 touchdowns, rushed for 810 yards and 14 touchdowns. He was selected to *Parade Magazine*'s All-American Team. During the recruiting process, he handled himself very well, and kept an open mind about what school he would attend.

He told me, "Coach, I want you to help me in my decision because you know how to talk to the coaches." I appreciated his vote of confidence in me, but I felt that since he and his family had been through the recruiting process with Michael, this time around with Marcus they would know how to deal with it. He visited the University of Miami, University of Virginia, University of Tennessee, and Virginia Tech. It became clear that Marcus would attend Virginia Tech when their quarterback coach, Rickey Bustle, resigned to become the new head coach at the University of Louisiana at Lafayette. This coaching change pleased Marcus, Michael, and me because we did not like some of the offensive strategies that Coach Bustle used or did not use with Michael as his quarterback. Coach Beamer hired a new quarterback coach named Kevin Rogers, who came to Virginia Tech from a fine career as Syracuse University's quarterback coach. He was well known for being a player's coach and helped develop NFL quarterback Donovan McNabb at Syracuse. He was well received by us because he had tried to recruit Michael to go to Syracuse, and we had gotten to know and like him.

The question most frequently asked about Marcus is, is he as good as Michael? How does he feel to be walking in his brother's footsteps at Virginia Tech? He has said, "I have always followed my brother. He is someone I admire, so I am honored to be compared to him, but I am even more excited to have an opportunity to attend the same school he did."

The jury is out on him as far as his talents are concerned. The door is wide open for him to play as a true freshman, something his brother did not do. However, I predict he will be a great player for the Hokies.

Jayson Vittori

There are athletes with physical talent. Some are blessed with unbelievable heart. Others are intelligent and use their savvy to succeed. Very few bring the best of all worlds together; Jayson is just such a student athlete.

Jayson Vittori's proud father introduced me to the five-six, 135-pound young man in the summer of 1997. Despite Jayson's size, his father was eager to see Jayson involved with football. Admittedly, I could not see this young man succeeding in our program, and certainly not at quarterback. With Dontrell Leonard shaping up as our junior varsity triggerman and Marcus Vick coming on board the following year, there would be no room for this blond-haired, blue-eyed, thirteen-year-old boy who looked more like a skateboarder than a football player.

Warwick Football is a select program, but we open the door to everyone. Those who choose to work hard will find other doors to pass through. Little did I know at the time, but my finest scholar athlete had just entered the house. During his freshman year, Jayson had to overcome the "step-up" shock. He had last played in a 120-pound maximum weight youth football program, and was one of our smallest players. He had decent speed, but his size was a negative factor. Nevertheless, we chose to play him at safety. Despite playing only 10 to 12 plays in his first game, he came up with a key interception for his JV team. I began to notice his intensity, and gradually I increased his playing time. Near the end of the season, I chose to bring Dontrell up to varsity level to gain exposure and to work with senior quarterback Michael Vick. Jayson became the heir apparent and quarterbacked the last three games. He played well, but I knew that he would not be able to compete with Marcus Vick the following year. Jayson understood, and the next season he moved to wide receiver. This was not a hard decision. It became readily apparent that the young man had exceptional hands. Rarely do you find someone at that age who can position his hands away from his body. I knew I had something special when I saw him pull in a Michael Vick "rocket" throw during a practice.

In his sophomore year, Jayson became Marcus Vick's favorite target. They were a lethal combination as they tore through the JV ranks. He underwent a growth spurt and was nearly six feet tall. His work in the weight room was also paying off. Near the end of the season, I moved him up to varsity. I saw a great deal of potential in this young man. Andre Harrison, my star All-American receiver, was graduating, and Jayson along with Marcus Vick would fill the void at receiver the following year.

With most of my players, I had to spend a great deal of time focusing them on academics. However, Jayson wasn't just intelligent, he was scary-smart. He was ranked second in his class and was enrolled in the school's rigorous International Baccalaureate program. There was no question about his SAT scores. The challenge became how to get him into an institution that would nurture both his athletic and academic skills. The Ivy League was a good fit, but he had Division 1A talent and his parents were hoping for a scholarship.

Jayson entered his junior year as a relative unknown in the state's powerful Peninsula District. About one-third of the way into the season, he was leading the league in pass receiving yards and catches. His amazing hands led to a series of circus-acrobat catches, culminating with an unbelievable over-the-shoulder diving grab against Gloucester High School. He was named First Team All-District. He entered his senior year with tremendous hope. Jayson was now six-three and 180 pounds. Marcus Vick would become his quarterback.

Despite Jayson's success, I had trouble getting the big colleges to look at him. We all face prejudice in some form throughout our lives. Most often I have seen this in regard to Blacks or other minorities. As a tall, white receiver with 4.6-second forty-yard dash times, he was typecast as a "possession" receiver—a Dwight Clark or Ed McCaffrey type. For one-tenth of a second, these schools were willing to overlook his tremendous talent and potential. I could sell him to smaller Division 1A schools and give him a chance to shine on the field, but Jayson's parents wanted him in a strong academic institution. Once again, we focused on the Ivy League.

Jayson's senior year was much like the previous one. He and Marcus led the league in receiving and passing. He was named first team All-District, All-Region, and All-State, and was selected to the *PrepStar Magazine* All-American teams. I was so proud of this young man. Not only is he a great football player, he is also like a son to me. He gave the program everything he had, and he was always the last one to leave the practice field. He played hurt, and he ran the tough routes over the middle knowing that he was going to get hammered. And he was smart, both on the field and off. Sometimes, I thought he knew the offense better than I did. He kept the team straight in the huddle. In the classroom, there were few who could compare with him. His acceptance to Harvard made me very proud. He was the second football player from my program to enter an Ivy League school.

Once Jayson enrolled at Harvard University, the head football coach considered him a prize catch. Harvard does not offer athletic scholarships thus Jayson competed for a series of merit scholarships, and was able to garner the highly prestigious Eddie Robinson

Scholarship for student athletes. I felt a great deal of gratitude to have played a role in Jayson's recognition by one of the best-ever college football coaches, who happens to be black. Perhaps he had nothing to do with it, but I choose to believe that it was Eddie Robinson who could see beyond color and recognize the value of this special young man.

Jayson received several other awards, including a Joint Resolution by the Virginia General Assembly recognizing him for community service. He was also awarded the Henry Jordan Memorial Scholarship,

Coach Reamon and Jayson Vittori at Jayson's last game for Warwick High.

given to Warwick High School's top scholar athlete. Jayson was the class salutatorian, and during his commencement address, he discussed how special it was to play for me and within my program. I have received many forms of thanks ranging from handshakes to expensive gifts. None has touched me like his words. Thinking back on Jayson as that scrawny young boy, little did I know he would develop into the finest scholar-athlete I have ever known. It was like discovering that proverbial diamond in the rough.

11. Today's Journey

It has become clear to me that one of my most important roles as a high school coach is helping develop life skills in my players. I define "life skills" as those mental, emotional, and social characteristics and behaviors that athletes develop or refine through their participation in football. Teamwork, leadership, the ability to set and achieve goals, discipline, emotional control, and good moral values are just a few. Today, more than ever before, there is a need for positive youth development in our society. Increasing drug use, youth violence, lack of parental involvement, and teen pregnancy are but some of the obstacles that are faced by today's youth. However, kids do not have to fall victim to these circumstances.

In this chapter I will discuss various experiences I have had with my student athletes, and answer questions that often come up at coaches' clinics on the strategies I use in the guidance and development of student athletes. I will also give a number of strategies that any teacher or coach can use to foster the development of life skills in their student athletes. I ask the parents of all my players to think about what benefit the student can derive from participation in my program, and I believe that taking part in athletics is one of the most important parts of any educational experience. There are few courses in our schools today that can offer all the following benefits the way that athletics can:

Competition—Our entire way of life is based on competition. Every person is competing to improve or maintain his standing: in a career, with regard to money, even in social situations. What better way to learn this important principle than through athletics?

Physical Well-Being—The nation is becoming more conscious of the poor physical fitness of our youth. Athletics builds a foundation that can correct this problem and help lead to a healthier adulthood.

Release of Physical Energy—Some way, somehow, students will find a way to release their energy. Athletics offers a wholesome outlet for this purpose, and a better alternative to the all-too-familiar teenage wildness that only leads to trouble.

Recognition—With guidance, players can learn to accept recognition in a proper manner. They learn that the praises they receive are not due to their efforts alone, that they play on a team, and the team concept should reinforce what the family at home teaches. The recognition and praise they receive could come from their entire supporting cast: family, teammates, coaches, teachers, and friends. By receiving praise from one another, they begin to build an even stronger self-image, and work harder to maintain that positive self-image. Likewise, receiving praise also teaches them to give praise.

Understanding—Players working together for a common cause learn how to accept victory or defeat in a mature manner. Team members soon learn how to understand each other and make adjustments for the good of the team.

Emotional Control—The athlete learns to get along and stay focused by tackling the task at hand. She or he learns to control the emotional blow-ups that only hamper her or his performance.

Discipline—We hear the cry that young people need to learn discipline. Athletics teaches self-discipline, which is vital to a successful adult life.

Perseverance—Athletes learn to stay with the job until it is done.

Thinking under Pressure—The accomplished businessman can attribute much of his success to this ability. Athletes learn it early in their careers and use this ability the rest of their lives.

Loyalty—Being faithful to a team, a group, a cause is an important lesson of athletics. A person will not fail himself when he has learned the lesson of being true to others.

Questions and Answers

How do you pick a potential scholarship athlete?

The observation and evaluation of these athletes begins at the middle school age. I observe them through community recreation leagues, AAU basketball teams, and my high school teams. I seek the most aggressive and athletic players who appear to have good attitudes. I seek students who perform well in the classroom, and when they do not perform well, which is the case with 70 percent of these kids, I request help and information from parents and teachers. Today, college football coaches have boiler-plate skills that they look for to fill certain positions, like physical size, speed, and agility. Since the college recruiters dictate what they want, I attempt to specialize my players to meet the recruiters' needs. Just like in the world of business, the consumer dictates the products that a business produces. The positions on my team that have had the greatest success in being awarded a scholarship are the quarterback, wide receiver, running back, defensive back, and linebacker. The linemen on the team are usually not tall enough, yet they may meet the requirements for smaller academic colleges.

What kind of students get athletic scholarships?

It's my personal belief that all athletes possess the ability to be scholarship athletes. However, there are different types of student athletes who fit the bill in different ways. First, there are athletes who are just naturally talented, who possess natural abilities to effortlessly play just about any sport known to man, and can perform with little guidance. Michael Vick and Aaron Brooks fit well into this category. Then you have the student athletes who have a high level of knowledge of the sport, but have yet to develop the fundamentals or techniques to the level necessary in order to become highly successful, and I think Kwamie Lassiter is an excellent example of this type. Finally, you have student athletes who are not naturally talented and who are not knowledgeable of the sport, but are coachable. They're hard workers, dedicated, fast learners, natural-born leaders, and have the desire to excel, and most important, are often good students. Jayson Vittori would be the best example of this type.

In any of these cases, there is potential for a scholarship athlete, but it's up to the coach to develop the athlete's talent to the level needed in order for him or her to emerge as a potential scholarship athlete.

In my fourteen years of coaching, the 2000 and 2001 football teams were the most unique groups of twenty-one scholarship athletes. The two teams had a combined 15-5 win-loss record. The 2000 team recorded my best win-loss record as a coach, and the 2001 team earned the program's first state playoff appearance. Each athlete on these teams entered the program as a freshman, and in his senior year was awarded a football scholarship. Each one of them had his own story. Each one had a personal relationship with me. I knew what they needed and I wanted to help them touch their dreams. In any group of students, there are those who stand out among the others, but in this group, all were exceptional.

They all bought into my concept of goal-planning, which I thank them for. They all wanted the opportunity to go to college and pursue a trade, career, or training to make their lives better. It is an honor for me to name these student athletes and the colleges they attended, and I thank them all:

Tyrus Lassiter, Terrell Johnson, Dontrell Leonard, and Kevin Talley—Norfolk State University.

Casey Tucker—Butler County, Kansas Junior College.

Terrance Hogan, Jarod Peay—Virginia State University.

Bernardo Richardson, Andrew Henderson—The Citadel.

Cameron Muro, Scorpio Brown, Joshua Mangana—Hampton University.

Antoine Andrews, Ben Brown—Christopher Newport University.

Nathaniel Manning—Kent State University.

Brandon Diggs—U.S. Naval Academy.

Adam Mangana—Brown University.
Melvin Massey—University of Virginia.
Jayson Vittori—Harvard University.
Brenden Hill, Marcus Vick—Virginia Tech.

What are the responsibilities of a gifted athlete's family?

The family has to be supportive. The parents should educate themselves about the process that a student athlete must go through from the
moment he or she enters the ninth grade. There is much written about
the process, all readily available from the school or on the Internet. The
parents who believe their child is gifted should also know as much as
the coaches. I welcome communication with parents who want me to
educate them about their child's experience. A potential scholarship
athlete must also have his or her parents' support in meeting the many
NCAA recruiting guidelines if he is to win a scholarship.

What do you do to have a good relationship with parents?

With a little effort, you can have parents working with you and
appreciating your efforts. Inform parents about the nature of the sport
and its potential risks. Allow parents to become acquainted with you,
the person responsible for their child. Explain team rules, regulations,
and procedures. Obtain help from parents in conducting the season's
activities, and let parents know what is expected of the athletes and of
them.

How do you deal with parental problems?

Coaches should expect to spend time on these issues. Two
types of parent problems are most common. First, some parents of
players are overly involved in their children's football experience.
They constantly criticize their son's play, your coaching, and the
officials' performance. In one game, a father's inappropriate
behavior led to an altercation with fans from the opposing team.

Rough Diamonds

In another game, a parent started yelling at *me* because he was unhappy with his son's play. The opposite problem is under-involvement—parents who play a very small role in their children's lives. The best way to deal with either of these problems is to stop them before they start.

While holding a parent meeting will solve many problems, it will not eliminate them all. There are some over-involved parents who will confront you. The key to dealing with these potentially volatile situations is to stay in control of your emotions and think before you speak. Do not enter into confrontations with parents on the field or around the athletes. It is best to schedule a meeting away from the field and the emotions of the game. Always stop and take a deep breath. Think of all your choices. Anticipate the consequences of each choice, and respond with the best one.

Working with under-involved parents also has its difficulties. One strategy is to give them a phone call to follow up on any letters that you have sent, or that an academic teacher may have sent. Talk to them about their son and how they might support his involvement. For example, talk about his game if they cannot attend. If they seem detached and uninterested, you might consider monitoring their son more carefully and providing more adult guidance. This child may need an adult mentor who cares.

Unfortunately, coaches will always have to deal with parental problems, and there is no indication that these problems are going away. In fact, they appear to be on the rise.

As mentioned, you should hold a parent meeting prior to the start of the season. We have our meeting the Saturday morning prior to the team's first intersquad scrimmage. At the meeting, you should

- introduce yourself and coaching staff,
- explain your objectives for the program and your philosophy of coaching,
- briefly cover football rules and regulations,
- indicate when and where parents should contact you if they have concerns or questions,

- specify your policy on playing time,
- clearly set out how parents can help their child be successful,
- discuss team/school rules regarding eligibility, and
- have the parents sign a code of good conduct.

How do you handle racial differences among players?

It never takes long to see the racial tension among black, white, or other minority players on the team. In the locker room, talk to the players about how good the team can be during the season if they play together as a team. Tell them what you will do to bring them together and respect each other's differences. Give a strategy—for instance, have all the players sit together during lunch at an assigned table for football players only. Discuss how the team's full potential will only be met if everyone's talents are utilized. Also, emphasize the importance of each one's cultural background, and help them learn to appreciate different backgrounds. Let them know you judge them only on how they act, their behavior on and off the field. Above all, make it very clear you will not tolerate racial prejudice of any kind, that an act of prejudice will be disciplined; and reinforce appropriate behaviors.

How do you deal with a player who shows bad sportsmanship?

Let's say a potential scholarship player plays linebacker. He always gives you his best effort and loves to play the game. However, he often takes his competitive spirit too far and gives cheap shots or late hits, and constantly engages in trash talk.

See if this sounds familiar: The first game of the season, on the second play of the game, he tackles the quarterback for a sack. The next play he intercepts a pass, and on the return run he gets tackled hard as he goes out of bounds. Everything is clean and legal, but he starts yelling at the officials and cursing at the opposing team's bench. He receives a 15-yard unsportsmanlike conduct penalty.

What do you do? Hold an individual meeting with him and let him know how much you appreciate his desire to win and overall competitiveness. Indicate, however, that this competitive spirit does him and the team little good if he is sitting on the bench or the team gets a penalty. The issue is for him to maintain his competitive spirit while learning to control his emotions. Let him know that, while some high-level players engage in trash talk and taunting because they think it is "cool," you do not think it is a classy way to act. Remind him that if a potential college coach sees him display that kind of behavior, he can forget that recruiter because he just turned him off and away.

How do you assist your players with their academic achievement?

Many of our players love to play football, but they show little interest in their schoolwork. In fact, many of these boys could drop out of school, and their futures would be doomed. Several others could get the opportunity to go to college and play football if they stayed on top of their schoolwork. You should devise a plan for helping your players combat lack of interest and stay on top of schoolwork. From the first day of practice, emphasize the importance of schoolwork and the possibility of being declared ineligible if their grades are not up to par. Take the time to have the players set some goals in this area. Set up an after-school study period. My team does not go out on the football field for practice until the study period is over. Players are allowed to get tutoring from their regular teachers and go to the library for special projects. Send out a weekly progress report to all of the teachers. Be consistent in your interest in the players' academic development.

The First and Ten Mentoring Program

The First and Ten mentoring program was designed by former professional football player turned educator Oliver W. Spencer, Ph.D. I have implemented the First and Ten Mentoring Program and highly recommend this resource to assist your students. It uses a creative blend of practical and scholarly strategies, proven to help at-risk young men be thoughtful about their futures and set realistic short- and long-term goals. The program uses the familiar concept of making a "first down" as a tool to help them set and meet these goals. By approaching life challenges as they would on the football field, they set realistic, stepwise goals and achieve them, just like they march toward the end zone—ten yards at a time. The program is designed for all students from kindergarten through their senior year in high school, and can be started anywhere with the help of Dr. Spencer's course materials.

Michael Vick, himself a graduate of the First and Ten Program, along with Dr. Spencer.

Rough Diamonds

It outlines the procedures necessary to run a First and Ten Mentoring Program in your local school district, and is divided up into sections for mentors, school staff, parents, and students. Each section contains information about the specific components of the program as it applies to the group under discussion, and samples of the official First and Ten forms to be used by that group.

The mentor training includes sample lesson plans that can be adapted to motivational and self-esteem-building materials, including:

- behavior management—where mentors assess the individual student's weekly progress
- social relations—where mentors discuss issues such as drugs and alcohol, cultural diversity, gangs, sports, and so forth
- daily reading—at home and at school, including a book report format to help in the development of comprehension skills
- tutoring sessions held with students in subjects identified by their teachers as needing assistance

Just as a football team rotates through specialty drill stations while practicing or warming up for a game—some on the sleds, some on the tackling dummies, some on the obstacle course, some on passing or kicking, and so on—the First and Ten organizes small teams to rotate through stations that cover the four components of the program each half-hour, and complete all activities within a two-hour period.

Each student's progress is measured by gaining "yardage points." The objective is for each student to gain a minimum of 1,000 yards by the end of the ten-week program. Yards are gained by reading every day, improving attendance, showing good citizenship, and academic achievement in school. Mentors work with the students for 90 minutes each week in regular sessions. At the end of each program, an Awards and Recognition Banquet is held for parents and students.

The First and Ten mentoring program represents everything I stand for as a coach in developing student athletes. I have watched my players grow to be better citizens and role models because of this

188

program. Many of them have learned to approach life as if it were a football game, and have struggled to gain inches and yards in order to score in many aspects of their young lives.

Two of my young players who adopted the First and Ten motto, "We Believe We Can Achieve," were the brothers Adam and Joshua Mangana. They spent a combined six years together in my football program. They were excellent student athletes. Dr. Oliver Spencer, the executive director of the First and Ten program, introduced them to it in middle school. Adam would regularly attend the meetings set up by the program's codirector, Mrs. Spencer. In his team's class he dealt with goal-setting, time management, and other life skills. After a year of participating in the tutorial component of the program's class, he often shared with me how helpful it was for him and other players. He understood and practiced the program's main goal that students must be well rounded. They must know how to fuse sports, academics, and citizenship. He became such an advocate for the program that he was made a full-time mentor in the program.

Success story: Principal Gene Jones, parents, and the 2000 team players and First and Ten program participants who were awarded scholarships.

During our football seasons, Adam coordinated the tutoring components with our football players. In after-school study periods, before practice, Adam volunteered to coordinate academic help between teachers and players. He recruited honor students in our school to help our student athletes in math, reading, and social studies. One of the students who benefited was Melvin Massey, now a scholarship football player at the University of Virginia. Melvin often told me how much Adam and the other First and Ten mentors helped him in his algebra class. Adam proved the old saying that "the best salesman for a product is the user of the product." He became a great mentor with a genuine desire to help others achieve. He often said to me, "Coach, because of my age, I can relate to many of our athletes' experiences better than an adult. The players respond positively to me." Today, Adam is a student athlete at Brown University. His younger brother, Joshua, took over the mentorship and brought along his teammates to continue the success of the program at my school.

Finally, the most powerful statement about the First and Ten program came from a former football player, Kevin Talley, who participated in it for two years. He is now a scholarship player at Norfolk State University. Kevin said, "To be a part of a team and develop that sense of pride and comradeship is important." The First and Ten program has helped my players achieve beyond the football field.

As important as programs like the First and Ten are in my arsenal of strategies, they are merely tools that help me get my job done. The most important skill that I can communicate in making a solid football program is still building links between players and the team. No set of tools, in and of itself, can take the place of those links, which can only be developed over time, with patience and careful planning, and most important, the willingness of the coach to share his players' dreams.

I have tried to communicate in this book the adventures in human relations I have experienced and those I have shared with the young men I have coached. If it had not been for the devastating pain of falling short of my career dreams, I would not be telling my story—

would not have made the impact I have on the lives of these few diamonds. A conversation I had with Michael Vick two days after his great performance in the national championship game against Florida State illustrates what I mean. We had dinner together one evening, and I told him of my experience in Hollywood and how I was forced to return home and become a coach. I said, "Michael I have given you and other players all the experiences of my life and fallen dreams. The dreams you've had since we met became my dreams for you. At times, I must have seemed obsessed with trying to help you and others not make the same mistakes. I hope I wasn't too unbearable."

He then delivered the most powerful response I could receive. He said, "Coach, if you had made that movie and not returned home, what would have happened to me? I wouldn't be where I am today."

Brooks hugs cousin Michael after a Newport News charity flag football game.